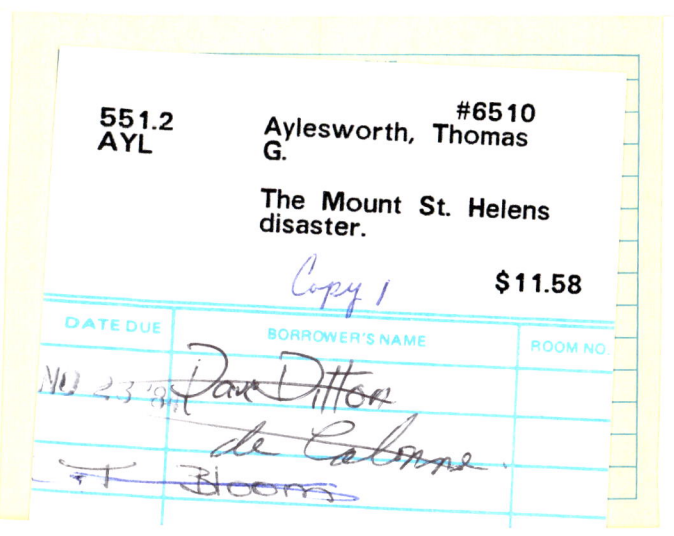

551.2 AYL Aylesworth, Thomas G.

The Mount St. Helens disaster.

Copy 1

**HOMESTEAD HIGH SCHOOL
LIBRARY MEDIA CENTER**

THE MOUNT ST. HELENS DISASTER

THE MOUNT ST. HELENS DISASTER

WHAT WE'VE LEARNED

THOMAS G. AND VIRGINIA L. AYLESWORTH

Franklin Watts
New York / London / Toronto / Sydney / 1983
An Impact Book

Cover photograph courtesy
of United Press International

Diagrams courtesy of Vantage Art, Inc.

Photographs courtesy of:
n.c.: p. 4-5;
U.S. Geological Survey: pp. 8, 16, 19;
United Press International:
pp. 20, 23, 26, 38, 56, 71, 74.

Library of Congress Cataloging in Publication Data

Aylesworth, Thomas G.
The Mount St. Helens Disaster.

(An Impact book)
Bibliography: p.
Includes index.
Summary: Describes the volcanic eruption of Mount St. Helens, and the close scientific monitoring concerned with recurrence, ecological impact, and weather changes.
1. Saint Helens, Mount (Wash.)—Eruption, 1980—
Juvenile literature. [1. Saint Helens, Mount (Wash.)—
Eruption, 1980. 2. Volcanoes] I. Aylesworth, Virginia L.
II. Title. III. Title: The Mount Saint Helens disaster.
QE523.S23A94 1983   551.2'1'0979784   82-20129
ISBN 0-531-04488-2

Copyright © 1983 by Thomas G. and Virginia L. Aylesworth
All rights reserved
Printed in the United States of America
5 4

CONTENTS

Chapter One
Out of the Past
1

Chapter Two
The Buildup
7

Chapter Three
The Blowup
15

Chapter Four
The Aftermath
25

Chapter Five
At What a Cost!
33

Chapter Six
Mopping Up
36

Chapter Seven
Scientists and Volcanoes
41

Chapter Eight
Volcanology and Mount St. Helens
55

Chapter Nine
Biology and Mount St. Helens
67

Chapter Ten
And After
73

Glossary
77

Bibliography
79

Index
83

For Allison and Art Boelter,
who survived,

and

to the memory of Harry R. Truman,
who didn't.

*"I have some people ask me why . . . I stayed.
That's my life—Spirit Lake and Mount St. Helens. . . .
I lived there 50 years—it's a part of me.
That mountain and that lake is a part of Truman.
And I'm a part of it."*

THE MOUNT ST. HELENS DISASTER

CHAPTER ONE

OUT OF THE PAST

Mount St. Helens, a long-dormant volcano, blew up on May 18, 1980. The whole northern face seemed to disappear; a jet of steam and ash shot almost 12 miles (19 km) into the sky; at the same time an earthquake, the equivalent of more than 10,000 tons of exploding TNT, rumbled through the ground. There had been warnings, of course, but who could have believed that such a beautiful mountain would suddenly become an angry opening on the surface of the earth?

What had it been like before the eruption? A serene lake sheltered by lush forest in the Gifford Pinchot National Forest in the state of Washington. A commanding, symmetrical, snow-capped mountain that dominated the skyline. These descriptions of Mount St. Helens are now just memories. They are landmarks of the Pacific Northwest forever changed by one of the most cataclysmic events witnessed on the continent of North America.

Mount St. Helens received its present name in 1792. Captain George Vancouver, a British explorer, christened the mountain "in honour of his Britannic Majesty's Ambassador at the Court of Madrid." He was referring to Baron St. Helens, who served as the British ambassador to Spain from 1790 to 1794.

But long before that, the Yakima Indians of the region called Mount St. Helens "Loo-Wit," meaning "Lady of Fire." There were numerous legends about the Lady of Fire.

One of them concerns the Great Spirit and his two sons. The Great Spirit was so pleased that the tribes of his two sons were friendly that he built a bridge across a wide river that lay between the territories of the two tribes. It was called the Bridge of the Gods. But eventually the tribes became selfish, greedy, and quarrelsome, and the Great Spirit took away the sun and their fire in order to punish them. When the winter came, the tribes had no fire to keep them warm.

Realizing their mistake, they prayed for fire. Their prayer so affected the Great Spirit that he went to the lodge of an old woman, Loo-Wit. Because she was pure in heart, she still had fire to keep her warm. The Great Spirit offered to grant her one wish if she would share her fire with the freezing Indians.

She vowed to take her fire to the bridge and promised to keep it burning forever so that it could be used by the people on both sides of the river. Then she made her wish: to become young and beautiful. Her wish was granted.

The next morning, Loo-Wit, now a handsome young woman, appeared at the bridge with her fire. The sun came out too, and the tribes promised to live in peace and harmony. But this was not to be.

The two chiefs, Wyeast and Klickitat, were struck by Loo-Wit's beauty, and both of them fell in love with her. When they asked her to choose between them, she refused because she loved both of them equally. Overcome by anger and jealousy, the chiefs declared war on each other. Many people in both tribes were killed, and the Great Spirit became angry.

He destroyed the bridge and turned the two chiefs into mountains. Wyeast became Mount Hood and Klickitat became Mount Adams. Although she was innocent of any wrongdoing, Loo-Wit was also transformed into a mountain—Mount St. Helens. But because of her innocence, the Great Spirit promised her that she would remain beautiful forever.

Other Indians claimed that Mount St. Helens and Mount Hood were once husband and wife, but they quarrelled and threw fire at each other. Mount St. Helens seems to have won the argument, because she continues to burn.

The Klickitat Indians called Mount St. Helens "Tah-one-lat-clah," which means "Fire Mountain." The Cowlitz tribe named it "Lawetlatla," or "Person from Whom Smoke Comes." Clearly, these legends and names suggest that Mount St. Helens had had a history of volcanic activity long before the arrival of white settlers.

Mount St. Helens' 1980 eruption, then, was not the first explosion of this volcano. One of the early settlers in the area, Dr. Meredith Gairdner, wrote home to Scotland about an eruption of Mount St. Helens that occurred in 1831.

In 1842, there was a violent eruption. The Reverend John H. Frost commented, "I observed a column of smoke to ascend from the northwest slope of Mount St. Helens. . . . Have learned since that ashes have been thrown out in great abundance, even as far as The Dalles [an Oregon town on the Columbia River south of Mount St. Helens]."

Another eyewitness to the event, John L. Parrish, reported "vast columns of lurid smoke and fire . . . which, after attaining a certain elevation, spread out in a line parallel to the . . . horizon, and presented the appearance of a vast table, supported by immense pillars of convolving flame and smoke."

Mount St. Helens and surroundings before the May 1980 eruption.

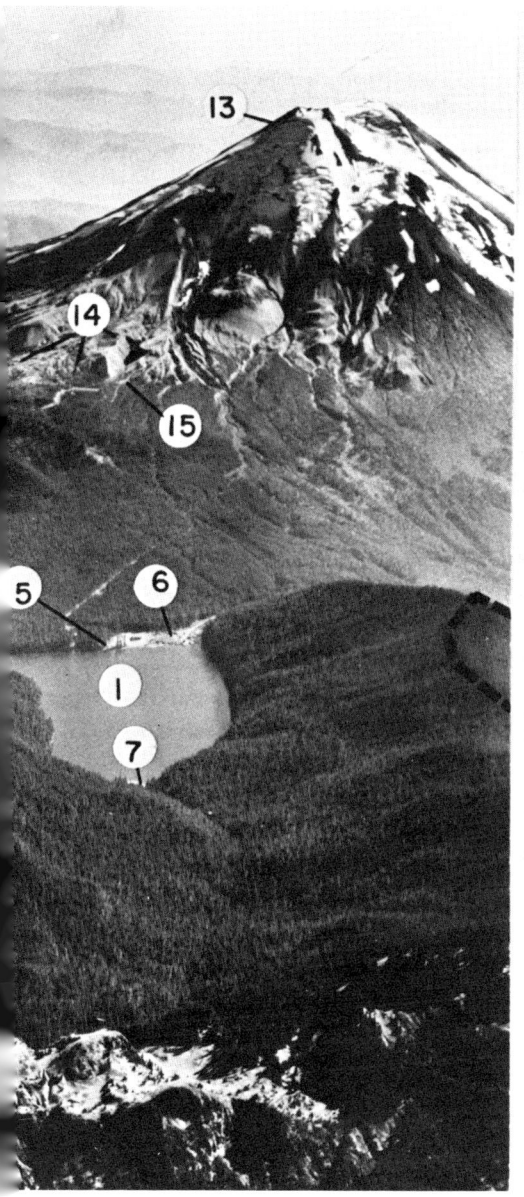

PHOTO NO. 67642

1. Spirit Lake
2. Duck Bay
3. Episcopal Church Organization Site (F.S.)
4. F.S. Administrative Site
5. Spirit Lake Recreation Development and V.I.S. Center
6. St. Helens Lodge
7. Bear Cove
8. F.S. Organization Sites
9. Portland YMCA Organization Site (Pvt.)
10. Harmony Falls Lodge (Pvt.)
11. Cedar Creek Campground
12. Donnybrook Campground
13. Mt. St. Helens
14. Timberline Winter Sports Site
15. Timberline Picnicground
16. Mt. Hood

The eruptions went on for fifteen years. In 1854 The *Portland Oregonian* reported that the crater "has been active for several days past. . . . Clouds of smoke and ashes are constantly rising from it. The smoke appears to come in puffs. . . . There is now more smoke issuing from it than there was a year ago, which indicates that the volcanic fires are rapidly increasing within the bowels of the majestic mountain."

The next eruption was in 1857. Then came a period of dormancy that lasted until a series of earthquakes and small eruptions began on March 20, 1980. According to scientists, the May 18 eruption was the most awesome explosion in the last thirty-five thousand years of Mount St. Helens' history. It killed sixty-two people, flooded one hundred forty homes, and flattened an entire hay crop and a valley full of trees. Two rivers were filled with so much debris that they had to be redug.

CHAPTER TWO

THE BUILDUP

Mount St. Helens is located 50 miles (80 km) north of Portland, Oregon, in the Gifford Pinchot National Forest in the state of Washington. Prior to the May 1980 eruption, it measured 9,677 feet (2,950 m) in altitude.

The first warning of the trouble to come occurred on Thursday, March 20, 1980. At 3:48 P.M., a *seismograph* (a device used to measure the intensity of earthquakes) needle jiggled at the United States Geological Survey (USGS) University of Washington headquarters. Data from this and other seismographs indicated that there was a sizable earthquake centered 20 miles (32 km) north of Mount St. Helens.

This earthquake registered 4.1 on the Richter scale. The Richter scale is a measure of ground motion. A reading of 3.5 would probably cause slight, localized damage. A reading of 5 means there has been a release of energy equivalent to an explosion of 1,000 tons of TNT. A reading of 7 is equivalent to 1 million tons of TNT. An 8 signifies a great quake that could cause tremendous damage. At the other end of the scale, a reading of 2 is about the smallest earthquake that could be felt by a human being.

A plume of light steam and ash erupts from Mount St. Helens on April 10, 1980.

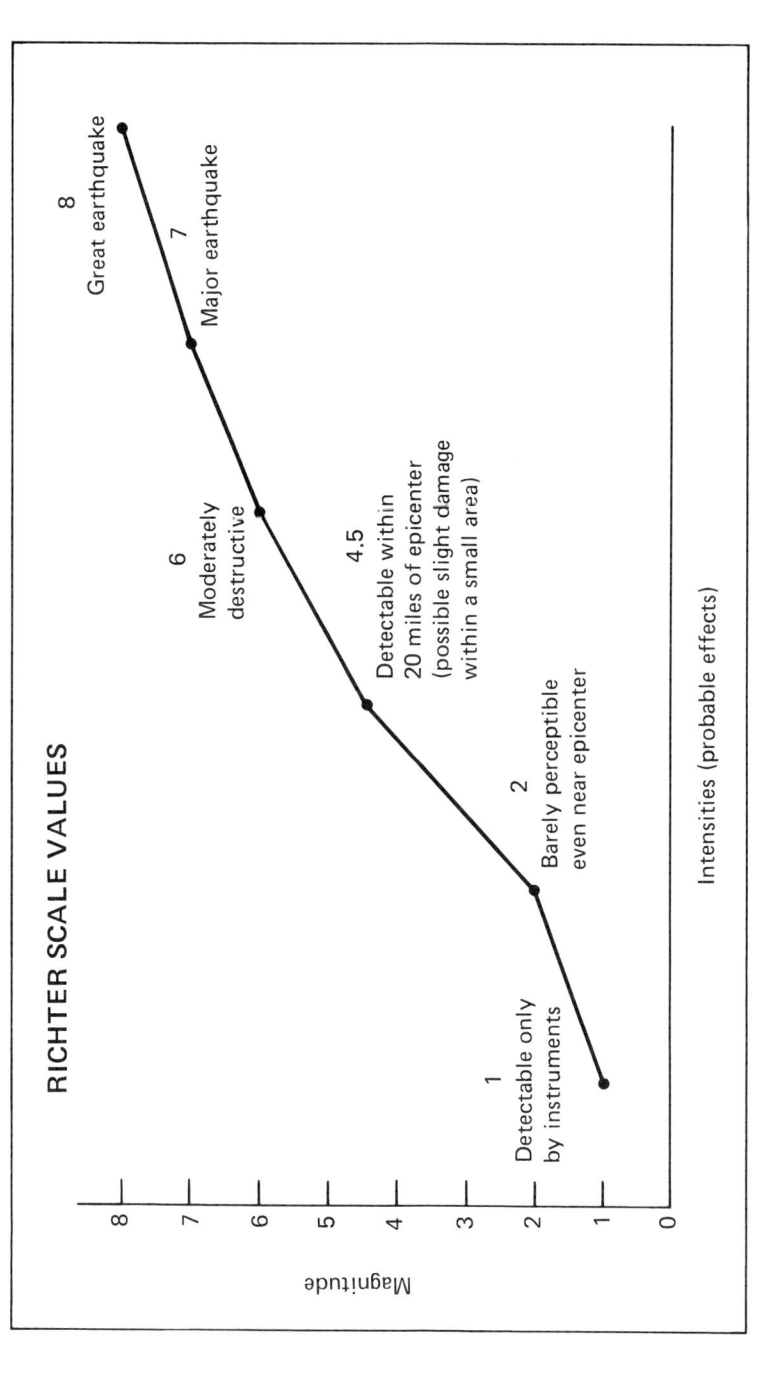

A scientist at the USGS station told of the experience. ". . . there had been a magnitude 4 earthquake reported by one of the permanent manned observatories east of the mountains, somewhere in western Washington. We spent about fifteen or twenty minutes ascertaining that the earthquake had been at Mount St. Helens. At about 4:30 in the afternoon we had a preliminary fix on the epicenter [the point on the earth's surface directly above the focus of an earthquake]. We had located it very shallow off the north side of the mountain."

At that time, there was no seismic coverage of Mount St. Helens, but the next day, machinery to measure *geothermal energy* (the heat below the surface of the earth) was put on the mountain.

Said one geologist, "Everything really broke loose on Monday here. . . . By Monday morning we had initiated attempts to keep track of the earthquakes, and initially we started to count earthquakes at the magnitude 2 level. By the end of the day that was no longer possible, because they were coming too many and too fast. We called the USGS in Denver—the volcano hazard people—and informed them that we had a major sequence earthquake going on that would have to be classified as volcanic."

By Tuesday, March 25, the number of earthquakes had hit a rate of forty per hour. On the afternoon of March 27, the mountain exploded, and a plume of ash and steam rose 4 miles (6.4 km) in the air. Also, a blemish appeared on the snow-capped peak—a black crater some 250 feet (76 m) wide and 60 feet (18 m) deep.

Geologists from several western states came to Vancouver, Washington. The USGS sent in a team of scientists. Officials planned evacuation procedures. Reporters from all over came to the site.

Even the students at Kelso Elementary School got into the act. They wrote a song that they sang to the tune of the theme of *The Muppet Show*:

*Let's get the lava flowing.
It's time to light the sky.
Let's get those ashes blowing
On Mount St. Helens tonight.
Boom, boom, boom, boom,
The crater's getting wider.
The mud is sliding fast.
The earth is shaking harder.
Oh, yeah, it's shaking harder
For the most sensational, irrigational,
  geographical, unpredictable.
This is the time for Mount St. Helens
  to blow!*

There were more eruptions the evening of March 27. They threw pulverized rock and steam into the night sky, up to a height of 4 miles (6.4 km).

By midmorning on March 28 a second crater appeared near the first. Eruptions continued to enlarge both craters until they joined to form a single crater 1,500 feet (460 m) wide, 2,000 feet (610 m) long, and 500 feet (150 m) deep.

A geologist, David Johnston, was working 4,300 feet (1,300 m) up the north side of Mount St. Helens. He reported, "It is extremely dangerous where we are standing. If the mountain exploded, we would die. It's like standing next to a dynamite keg with the fuse lit; only we don't know how long that fuse is."

On March 30, at 7:40 A.M., another eruption blew a cloud of ash and steam as far as Bend, Oregon, 150 miles (240 km) south. This was a *friatic eruption,* an eruption in which heat rises from the deep *magma,* or liquid rock, and melts the icy cap of the volcano so that a steam explosion occurs. This explosion also draws out volcanic ash that has been left over from previous eruptions.

That same day there were six more eruptions with ash clouds rising more than a mile (1.6 km) in the air.

Seven earthquakes were detected, ranging from 3.3 to 4.4 on the Richter scale.

On April 1, the earthquakes had escalated to readings of from 4.5 to 4.7. And on April 3 came the strongest quake yet—4.8—accompanied by *harmonic tremors*. A harmonic tremor is a constant vibration of the earth resulting from movement of magma deep beneath the volcano.

A state of emergency was announced by Governor Dixie Lee Ray. The United States Forest Service closed access roads, and the National Guard was called in to keep back sightseers.

The ash and steam continued to puff throughout April. Meanwhile, the north side of the summit began bulging out at the rate of about 5 feet (1.5 m) per day. That is rapid movement. A mountain usually expands no more than a fraction of an inch per year.

The scientists continued working. They analyzed the ash coming from Mount St. Helens, but they were more interested in what gases were being liberated than in the composition of the ash. And they were particularly interested in the amount of sulfur and chlorine in the gases. When magma moves up from deep within a volcano, the amount of sulfur and chlorine in the gases being liberated increases. But the scientists could see no clear trend.

On April 10, residents and workers were permitted to return to their homes and jobs in the area, but only after they had signed disclaimers, which stated that they recognized the risks and assumed responsibility for their own safety. That same day, Mount St. Helens erupted again, propelling a plume of light steam and ash 15,500 feet (4,700 m) above sea level. Seismic vibrations continued beneath the volcano. By this time the bulge on the upper north flank measured more than 320 feet (100 m). One hint that a huge eruption was coming would have been a sudden and extreme change in the bulge rate. But that didn't happen. Its growth remained gradual.

On April 13, a team of scientists flew in by helicopter to observe Mount St. Helens' swelling lava dome (the rounded uplift caused by the expansion of the lava). Although seismic activity had lessened, an eruption advisory remained in effect because it was thought that seismic activity could increase. The U.S. Forest Service announced that two zones around that mountain were to be closed to keep people at least 20 miles (32 km) away.

When the scientific team returned from their exploratory helicopter flight, they reported that glowing molten rock was moving within the crater. They had also watched the molten rock growing into a mound, adding to the existing dome of hardened lava.

Meanwhile, people began selling T-shirts imprinted with such inscriptions as "Mount St. Helens Is Hot," and "Survivor, Mount St. Helens Eruption—1980."

On April 24, scientists went into the crater on foot for the first time in five days. Clouds and rain had previously prevented them from flying to the crater. They measured expansions and contractions of the crater area and changes in the layers of volcanic ash.

Scientists reported on April 30 that the growing bulge was "the most serious potential hazard posed by current volcanic activity." Governor Ray then imposed restrictions that limited human access within 10 miles (16 km) of Mount St. Helens.

In May the situation grew more serious. On May 5, scientists confirmed that molten rock pushing up inside Mount St. Helens was causing the bulge. On May 7 there was another steam and ash eruption, followed the next day by an earthquake of magnitude 5. Another earthquake of the same magnitude was registered on May 9, and the USGS abandoned its observation installation at Timberline Camp at the 4,300-foot (1,300-m) level on the side of the mountain overlooking Spirit Lake. A University of Puget Sound geologist, Al Eggers, predicted a lava eruption on May 21.

On May 12, steam vents were observed along the crater's west rim, and a 5 magnitude quake set off an ice avalanche 800 feet (250 m) wide that slid for 3,000 feet (915 m) along the north face. Forty earthquakes were recorded on May 15. Despite the earthquakes and avalanche, Spirit Lake property owners made plans to re-enter the restricted area to recover their belongings.

On May 16, it was announced that residents were to be permitted back into the area. But Governor Ray gave them only four hours to pick up their possessions.

Geologist Dave Johnston was observing the mountain on May 17. He radioed back: "It could be in hours or even days or even a couple of months. But right now there's a very great hazard due to the fact that the glacier is breaking up on this side of the volcano—the north side. And that could produce a very large avalanche hazard. This is not a good spot to be standing in."

Livestock and wildlife seemed to sense the coming disaster. One farmer's wife told this story: "The pigs were squealing . . . so I figured they must be extra hungry. When I went out to feed them, Ruby [one of the hogs] was so excited that she jumped over the fence and ran around and around in circles. . . . And Wilbur [another hog] was squealing the whole time, too, and I had to chase them for an hour."

One 83-year-old man defied the mountain and the governor's orders and became a national hero. He was Harry R. Truman, and he had run a lodge at Spirit Lake for some fifty years. When he was told to leave, he said, "No one knows more about this mountain than Harry, and it don't dare blow up on him. No, I won't leave. They'll have to take me out of here. They'll have to come and get me."

At 8:32 A.M. on May 18, a ham radio operator heard David Johnston broadcasting. "Vancouver! Vancouver!" Johnston shouted into the radio. "This is it. . . ." Those were his last words.

CHAPTER THREE

THE BLOWUP

At ten seconds past 8:32 A.M. on May 18, Mount St. Helens exploded. The explosion was triggered by an earthquake that read 5.1 on the Richter scale. The northern face of the volcano, the side with the bulge, collapsed and slipped down the mountainside. A plume of steam shot from the peak, turning black in a matter of seconds, and rose 63,000 feet (19,200 m) in the air.

The explosion was heard 200 miles (320 km) away. Hot gas, ash, and huge rocks were hurled into the sky. The blast was estimated to have been five hundred times greater than the 20-kiloton atomic bomb that destroyed Hiroshima.

Searing hot *nuées ardentes*, or glowing avalanches, cut a swath that was more than 12 miles (19 km) wide and 5 miles (8 km) long through the forests that surrounded the volcano. Hurricanelike winds, traveling at rates of up to 200 miles (320 km) per hour, accompanied the blast, felled millions of two-hundred-year-old trees, and left animals that survived in a state of shock.

A plume of volcanic ash rose 48,000 feet (14,600 m) above the mountain, creating violent lightning displays that caused widespread forest fires. Fortunately, the falling ash put most of the fires out.

An avalanche of rocks, dirt, and debris fell slowly at first. But later it combined with melting snow, ice blocks, and water in the Toutle River, forming *lahars* (volcanic mudflows) whose velocity at times reached 50 miles (80 km) per hour and whose temperature was measured at 211°F (99°C). The lahars bulldozed the waters in the river, creating a massive wave 33 feet (10 m) high which plunged downstream for over 12 miles (19 km). It swept away logging camps, destroyed bridges, buried houses, and produced a flood that was packed solid with trees torn from the surrounding valley.

The mud avalanche poured into the South Fork of the Toutle at first, then into Spirit Lake, and then into the North Fork of the Toutle. There it formed a dam of logs, mud, and debris at the head of Spirit Lake that measured 200 feet (61 m) in height.

Meanwhile, hot ash and gas formed a pyroclastic flow that roared down the mountain slope at 100 miles (160 km) per hour, pouring over the debris that had already been deposited. This flow, registering temperatures of up to 800°F (425°C), became a superheated river of mud that traveled down the Toutle River to the Cowlitz River and the Columbia River. When the flow hit the Columbia River, new sand bars were thrown up that stranded freighters upriver in the port of Portland, Oregon. On land, the pyroclastic flow flipped 100-ton trucks into the air and destroyed a locomotive.

By afternoon the Toutle River registered 90°F (32°C), and at the point where it flowed into the Cowlitz River, it was 80°F (27°C)—hot enough to kill all the fish. The level of the Cowlitz was raised 15 feet (4.6 m) in some places.

Mount St. Helens erupts, May 18, 1980.

Helicopters rescued some one hundred fifty people during the hours after the blast, and more than a thousand were eventually evacuated.

The ash posed a severe problem. It was estimated that more than a cubic mile (4 cu km) of debris was thrown from the mountain—that is 1 ton of debris for every person on earth. Much of this debris was in the form of acid ash. When the ash began to fall from the sky, it accumulated to a depth of 0.6 inches (1.5 cm) as far away as 500 miles (800 km). Since the wind was blowing east, the eastern part of Washington was hardest hit. The town of Yakima alone received about 800,000 tons of the ash.

Ash closed roads in eastern Washington, bringing that part of the state to a standstill. It fell so quickly that automatic street lighting switched on because of the darkness. Airline flights were halted. Cars, buses, and trucks were unable to move. Some schools and businesses were closed as far away as Idaho, and roads in Montana were closed because of the poor visibility.

What was it like to live through this ash shower? Here is a story as told by a Seattle attorney, Arthur H. Boelter, Jr., who had traveled to a Washington State Bar Association seminar in the Tri-Cities of Richland, Pascoe, and Kennewick. The Tri-Cities are north and east of Mount St. Helens and on the eastern side of the Cascade Mountains.

"As I walked out of the door of the hotel, I noticed that the southwestern sky in the direction of the volcano was extremely black. I assumed that the cloud was a

Melting ice and snow created a river of mud that swept down the slopes of Mount St. Helens.

thundercloud. As it turned out, that black cloud was nothing but ash.

"Suddenly I noticed what appeared to be snow coming down. I could see it in the distance and cars were beginning to kick it up in the air. Of course I realized that it wasn't really snow, but some sort of flying powder. When I got to my car, I could see that there was a fine film all over it. It looked a bit like white flour.

"At the hotel, people seemed to be coming out of the woodwork. Everyone who was on some sort of camping or vacation trip headed to any hotel or motel that they could find. People began driving up in droves and checking in. Very soon the hotel was filled to the brim. When I got to my room, I turned on the TV and learned that it wasn't a good idea to go outside and breathe this stuff. Early reports said that the dust could have a bad effect on one's lungs.

"Throughout most of that day I could see that the dust cloud was getting heavier and heavier. Vision was restricted to about 100 feet [30 m] from my hotel room window. My first thought was that this whole thing would blow over in a couple of hours and perhaps I would be able to check out by early morning and head back home. But as I listened to the television, it became clear that this volcanic dust was clogging up the roads and closing them down all over the place. There were all sorts of conflicting reports about what roads were closed, but there was no conflict as to the amount of devastation that had been caused."

Longview, a small town near Mount St. Helens, was covered with a gray cloud of ash a few days after the eruption.

The ash from the Mount St. Helens eruption was a combination of powdery rock and glasslike fragments. Cars and buses kicked it up in the air. The ash clogged engines, reduced visibility, and forced drivers off the road. Over 2 inches (5.1 cm) covered Ritzville, a small farming community in central Washington.

The mayor of Ritzville commented: "You couldn't believe what it was. It was like a dust storm, but yet it was falling like snow. It was kind of like flour and you'd walk in it and it would sound kind of hollow, and you'd step in it. A lot of people said that it was like walking on the moon."

The population of Ritzville doubled. Two thousand motorists staggered in through the dust, their cars strewn along Interstate 90. The mayor continued: "We put them in the churches and the schools and food was taken from the grocery stores up to the schools by rescue teams that were set up through the sheriff's office. And then the volunteer fire department started dispatching the food, medicine, toothpaste, toothbrushes, anything that the people needed."

But what of those who had been the closest to the disaster and yet lived? One of the survivors described it this way: "The ash was kind of warm. It was warm all around us. I'd inhaled so much of it, it got down my throat. I swallowed a lot of it and I had to dig it out of my mouth just to be able to talk. My fingertips got burned—blistered."

The area where Harry R. Truman's Spirit Lake Lodge once stood, dotted with fumaroles shortly after the eruption, resembled the moon's surface.

Boelter continued his story: "It was interesting to watch the national news show pictures of what was happening and to know that what was going on was happening just a few short miles south of where I was. As soon as I knew that I would be in the hotel room overnight, I tried to call my wife, Allison, back in Gig Harbor. But all the Seattle-Tacoma lines were tied up. The operators simply could not get through. I continued to try to telephone off and on for two or three hours, it seems.

"When I did reach Allison, I said something like, 'Hi. How are you?'

"And she responded, 'Where are you? What are you doing? Why didn't you call me?'

"I said something like, 'Allison, what are you talking about? . . . The volcano blew its stack. . . .'

"She couldn't understand what I was talking about. She had been outside sunbathing and reading. There weren't any clouds in the sky over Gig Harbor because it lies west of Mount St. Helens. She hadn't heard any radio or television. She had no idea that the volcano had erupted."

The volcano roared all day on May 18, and most of the night. It spewed out no lava, just millions of tons of pumice, gas, and ash. By the next morning, 1,300 feet (400 m) of the peak of the mountain were missing from the southern rim, and 3,000 feet (914 m) were missing from the northern rim. The height of Mount St. Helens had been reduced from 9,677 feet (2,950 m) to 8,400 feet (2,560 m) at the southern rim and 6,800 feet (2,070 m) at the northern rim.

A steaming crater 1 mile (1.6 km) wide had appeared. The biggest landslide ever recorded had occurred when the bulge burst. Most of what had come out had been heated to near boiling temperatures and thrown into the valley. Harry Truman's lodge and Harry Truman himself were somewhere under the mud. Trees had been destroyed 20 miles (32 km) away. Spirit Lake had disappeared under 40 feet (12 m) of boiling mud.

CHAPTER FOUR

THE AFTERMATH

Almost immediately after the explosion, the Army, the Air Force, and the National Guard moved in to help, but there were problems. Each branch of the government (Army, Air Force, National Guard, Forest Service, etc.) had its own emergency radio frequency. For all of those groups to coordinate, a unified radio plan had to be set up. Later, an emergency radio frequency was announced, and this was used for contact only. Once a contact was made, the two parties could use another frequency. That allowed the emergency frequency to be kept clear and available to other broadcasters.

Then, too, pilot's maps had become obsolete overnight because of the change in the shape and size of the mountain. And there was no reliable list of people who were in the danger area. To clear up the difficulties, the Forest Service was put in command.

At the time, it was estimated that seventy people had been buried, suffocated by gases, or burned to death. But the most common cause of death was asphyxiation by ash. Two people died in a car going 70 miles (113 km) per hour, trying to outrace the ash cloud.

Forty-nine percent of Washington State received visible ash, and another 29 percent received deposits of 0.12 inches (3 mm) or more. The heaviest deposits

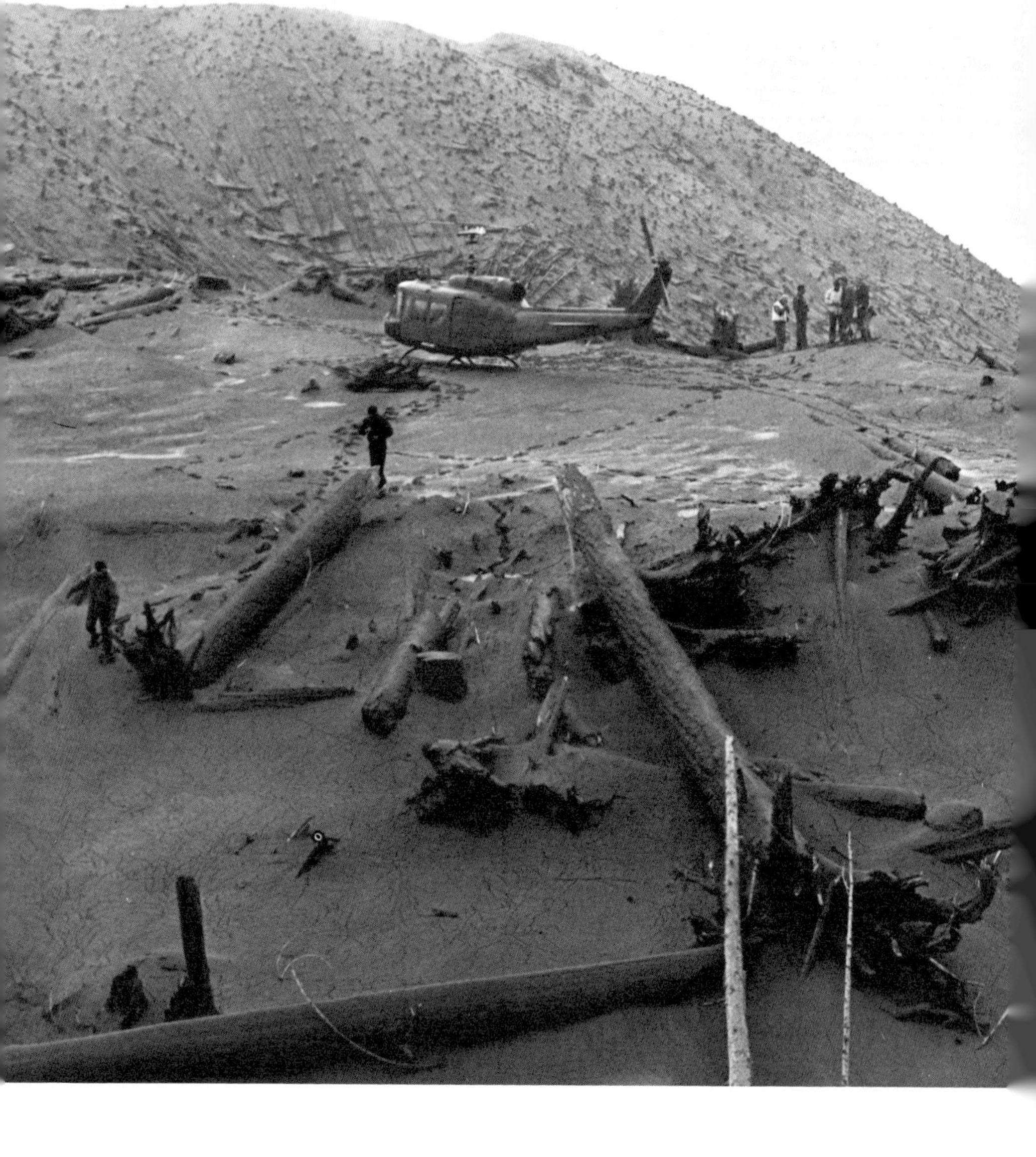

formed a layer 2 to 3 inches (5.1 to 7.6 cm) deep, and in some places it reached 6 inches (15.2 cm).

The 3M Company sent its entire stock of one million surgical masks to the state of Washington. Soon everyone was wearing masks, bandanas, coffee filters, or socks over his or her nose. A sign was put up in a Yakima bank that read: "For security purposes, please remove your masks before entering."

A resident of Spokane talked about the ash: "You wash it off your porches, sidewalks, and streets in the morning and by afternoon it's back. My neighbor washes his car every couple days, and it still looks like he drove it across the Sahara Desert. My bus driver's eyes are nearly swollen shut at night after driving for eight hours behind cars that kick up the ash."

Initially, there was a real worry about the volcanic ash that fell. Enough of it had fallen to cover 1 square mile (2.6 sq km) of the island of Manhattan to a depth three times the height of the Empire State Building.

It was feared that the fallout could cause cancer, human mutations, or silicosis (a lung disease), or aggravate allergies. Many of the particles of ash were so small that they could have been inhaled into the innermost parts of the human lung. But by September, studies made at the Batelle Memorial Institute's Northwest Laboratory indicated that the ash in the air would not harm the lungs of humans or do any damage to individual cells.

But scientists wondered about long-term effects the ash would have on the climate. The volcanic ash from

A U.S. Army helicopter crew searches for people reported missing after the eruption.

Mount St. Helens rose to the 70,000-foot (21,300-m) level and took only seventeen days to move entirely around the world. Volcanic ash in the atmosphere can dramatically change the climate of the world. For example, three major eruptions in the early nineteenth century were blamed for "the year there was no summer." Soufrière on St. Vincent Island erupted in 1812; Mayon in the Philippines erupted in 1814; and Tambora on the island of Sumbawa, Indonesia erupted in 1815. The year 1816 had freezing temperatures during mid-June in much of the northern hemisphere! Residents of the east coast of the United States dug themselves out of severe summer snowstorms. New England had crop-killing frosts in August. All of this was caused by the ash in the air depriving the earth of sunlight.

Although worried about the effects of the ash fallout, people kept their sense of humor. Some of them melted down the ash and made souvenir ashtrays. Others made ceramic salt and pepper shakers in the shape of the original Mount St. Helens. The top section that blew away was detachable from the lower part that remained. The top part held the pepper, and the lower part held the salt.

One disc jockey on a local station announced: "If you're planning on visiting Washington State this year, don't bother. Washington is coming to visit you."

The activity of Mount St. Helens declined during the days following the May 18 eruption. Seismic and eruptive events dropped to a level below that of late March. Then on May 25, a second major eruption occurred, consisting of steam and ash, although not as large as the one on May 18. This time the winds carried the ash south and west, spreading a thin layer over large portions of western Washington and Oregon.

The eruption of May 25 was followed by days of minor steam and ash plume eruptions and low-level seismic activity. Then Mount St. Helens erupted again on June 12, sending an ash column up 50,000 feet (15,250 m). This eruption lasted for six hours, and ash was deposited in the Portland-Vancouver area.

The June 12 eruption occurred at 8:45 P.M., and was Mount St. Helens' fourth major explosion. The noise was heard some 135 miles (217 km) away and was accompanied by harmonic tremors that began at 9:10 P.M. and lasted until 11:30 P.M., when they decreased considerably. They finally stopped at 9 A.M. the next morning.

The debris from this explosion was different from previous eruptions. It was darker in color and of a different chemical composition. This led scientists to suspect that it was coming from deeper in the volcano than the debris from the other eruptions. Fortunately, at the time of the fourth explosion, it was raining, and this confined the fallout of ash and dust.

By noon the next day, motorists in Portland, Oregon—70 miles (113 km) south—were forced to turn on their headlights, and people were putting on air filtration masks again. The cloud of ash hung over the city for three days.

On June 15, something new was observed on Mount St. Helens. It was a dome of extremely viscous, crusty volcanic lava, which seemed to have been exuded on the floor of the crater. Scientists suspected that the dome had been formed during the June 12 eruption but had remained undetected because of poor visibility for four days. At the time, it measured 700 feet (210 m) in circumference and was 130 feet (40 m) high. By June 18 it had doubled in height. Air observers said that it glowed in the dark. Pete Towley, a geologist with the USGS, said, "The glow is emanating from below, through cracks in the crust of solidified lava."

The dome grew as its upper surface cooled and cracked and as more hot material oozed upward. It was surrounded by a shallow moat of water that had trickled down from the inner walls of the crater. At the time, scientists thought that the dome would create a cone similar to Mount St. Helens' peak before the original eruption.

But restricted zones were closed again around Mount St. Helens on June 18. Scientists were predicting an immediate eruption, based upon their readings of low-frequency earthquakes that were pulsing through the volcano.

Shallow, low-frequency quakes had increased on June 17. They had been preceded by increased sulfur dioxide emissions and a deformation of the volcano's crater.

Predictions were that a dome-building eruption could be expected by June 20. The crater increased its swelling and also increased the number of shallow, volcanic earthquakes within the mountain.

The eruption occurred on June 19, pushing chunks of lava through cracks on the crater floor and adding to the size of the volcano's mammoth dome. It was a nonexplosive eruption. Scientists said that a leveling-out of seismic activity had diminished the chance of a more dangerous blast. This was the ninth eruption since the one of May 18, and the fourth nonviolent, dome-building eruption.

On July 19, a drop in the ratio of carbon dioxide to sulfur dioxide was detected in the gases coming from the crater. Scientists guessed that something was about to happen. On July 22, the dome was blown to bits at the start of a three-hour eruption. Fortunately, there had been a warning, and no one was hurt.

Two weeks later, the carbon dioxide–sulfur dioxide ratio fell again, and on August 7 a harmonic tremor was detected. A second dome, first observed on August 8, was destroyed by an eruption on August 16. A third dome was observed forming on October 18. A nonexplosive lava eruption occurred from December 17, 1980, to January 4, 1981, adding two additional lobes to the October domes. Nonexplosive eruptions on February 5, April 10, and June 18, 1981, added new extrusions to the preexisting composite dome.

On September 7, 1981, Mount St. Helens emitted a small plume of steam, but the earthquake activity had lessened. The lava dome had changed in shape, but no danger was predicted. Scientists who flew over the mountain at night reported glowing cracks crisscrossing the dome, while hot rocks gave off sparks as they fell into the crater.

Mike Doukas, a Geological Survey scientist, said, "It is like a big wart or bump on the side of the dome. At night it's pretty spectacular. There are ribbons and tongues of this glowing rock cascading down. You can see falling rocks coming down the slopes of the dome and exploding into sparks."

Activity on the mountain continued into 1982. On February 8 there was evidence that a new round of volcanic activity was in the works. Small earthquakes were registering, and the ground was deforming.

Then, at 7:28 P.M. on March 19, there was an explosive eruption. The scientists at the USGS Cascades Volcano Observatory in Vancouver had not expected such force. Neither had the University of Washington Geophysics Center, even though they had issued a warning at 9 A.M. that day predicting an eruption within twenty-four hours. Over the weekend of March 13 and 14, the mountain had been continuously shaken by very small earthquakes. On March 14 a 16,000-foot (4900-m) steam plume had risen in the air, and lava had been pushed from the dome inside the crater.

The March 19 blast shot an ash cloud to nearly 9 miles (14.5 km) above sea level, or 7 miles (11 km) above the top of the volcano. After about twenty-five minutes the activity slowed down.

Then, about six hours later, at 1:37 A.M. on March 20, there was a two-to-three-minute eruption in which the ash cloud rose 3 miles (4.8 km) into the air. Seismic activity then fell off, and the lava dome began to bulge slightly. By that night a new lobe of lava was forming on the top of the dome, and it began to ooze down the southeast flank of the mountain.

An avalanche of melted snow, mud, rocks, and ice plunged down the north side of the crater and split in two, with one part heading for the Toutle River and the other toward Spirit Lake. The part of the flow that headed for the Toutle measured 8 feet (2.4 m) in height and 660 feet (200 m) in width, and traveled at about 45 miles (72 km) per hour. Sixty-five people in the Toutle River area were evacuated, but the flow resulted in minimal damage—only the destruction of a few USGS instrument stations on the side of the mountain.

Scientists entered the crater on March 21 to study the lava dome and discovered that the activity seemed to be subsiding. Then, Mount St. Helens erupted again on April 4 and 5, and on April 6 blew steam and ash several miles into the sky. Gas emissions continued through the day on April 6.

Presently, Mount St. Helens remains calm with minor steam plumes and low-level seismic activity. The end of volcanic activity may still not be in sight. No one can predict if the mountain will stop erupting, continue in its present mode, or erupt more violently than it did on May 18, 1980. Only time will tell.

CHAPTER FIVE

AT WHAT A COST!

The May 1980 disaster at Mount St. Helens claimed many human lives. Thirty-five people were killed, and twenty-five were declared missing and presumed dead.

What happened to the farmers of the region? The eight counties in Washington that were the most affected had, in 1979, produced $1.4 billion in crops and $270 million in a combination of livestock and livestock products. That amounted to 65 percent and 38 percent, respectively, of the total state crop and livestock production. Crop losses from the disaster were estimated to be about $100 million, or about 7 percent of the normal crop value for that region.

The orchards and wheat fields of eastern Washington got most of the ash. Fifty percent of the alfalfa hay crop was ruined. On the other hand, even though the alfalfa crop was hit hard by the ash, the farmers found that their cattle could still eat the plants.

There was another bright side. The wheat, potato, and apple crops were normal or above normal, probably because of the decrease in the destructive insect populations. Indeed, in Cowlitz County, the wheat harvest was nearly twice that of a normal crop.

Animal	Number lost during initial eruption and from volcanic flows	Number lost as a result of ashfall
Elk	5,250	1,910
Black-tailed deer	6,000	6,180
Black bear	200	170
Mountain lion	15	— —
Mountain goat	15	— —
Forest and sage grouse	27,750	136,220
Hare	11,300	67,000
Jackrabbit	— —	54,000
Pigeon	8,500	— —
Pheasant	— —	440,000
Quail	— —	282,000
Hungarian partridge	— —	141,000
Yellow-bellied marmot	— —	67,000
Duck and coot	— —	160,000
Goose	— —	16,000
Morning dove	— —	65,000
Beaver	1,016	720
Muskrat	2,714	1,425
Otter	186	— —
Mink	504	355
Coyote	1,411	3,480
Raccoon	1,181	365
Marten	710	— —
Bobcat	300	75
TOTALS	67,052	1,483,900

Most plants tended to shed the ash; however, the ash did cause more breakdowns in farm equipment. The ash also reduced water infiltrations, increased the proportion of sunlight reflected back into space, and affected water runoff, erosion, evaporation, and soil temperature, all of which made farming in the area more difficult.

Not so lucky were the tree farmers. More than 100 square miles (260 sq km), or $100 million worth of timber had been destroyed. The Forest Service estimated that 3.2 billion board feet of timber was destroyed. But 600 million board feet was salvaged.

But the greatest loss was that of the wildlife in the area. Birds and insects burned up in the air or were suffocated by the ash which fell up to 2 feet (0.6 m) thick over hundreds of square miles, smothering animal and plant life on the ground. Mud and rocks cascaded down stream beds on Mount St. Helens, destroying everything in their paths. Superheated gas, combined with pulverized rock and ash, hurtled down the face of the mountain, killing all life and ending up in Spirit Lake and the nearby rivers, turning them into boiling cauldrons of mud and killing the water animals.

Scientists believe that at least 1.5 million game birds and mammals were lost as a result of Mount St. Helens' eruptions and subsequent ashfall. That does not include nearly eleven million salmon and other fish that were killed, or untold numbers of nongame animals, amphibians, and insects.

A table of the estimated awesome toll is on the facing page.

CHAPTER SIX

MOPPING UP

When President Jimmy Carter visited the disaster scene, he asked Governor Dixie Lee Ray what help the federal government could provide following the eruption of Mount St. Helens. She spelled it out, very slowly: "M-O-N-E-Y."

It was obvious that Carter was overwhelmed by the tragedy. He later said: "There was no way to prepare oneself for the sight we beheld. . . . I don't know that there's ever been in recorded history in our nation a more formidable explosion. . . . It's the worst thing I've ever seen. . . .

"I don't know how long it will take for that region to be opened even for normal movement of traffic. There are enormous blocks of ice apparently still covered by literally hundreds of feet of fluffy, face-powder-type ash, and as that ice is melted under the hot conditions that exist, enormous cave-ins are taking place. Steam is bubbling up; there are a few fires about.

"Someone said it was like a moonscape, but it's much worse than anything I've ever seen in the pictures of the moon's surface. Fortunately, the people in that region were minimal, but it is literally indescribable in its devastation."

The cleanup began almost immediately. Within three weeks, loggers had moved 15 million board-feet of fallen timber from the blast area to the mills.

The dangers were not over, however, for the loggers who had to go in and salvage the timber. One of their spokesmen said: "It is the most dangerous kind of cutting, with logs lying on top of each other . . . you could cut one piece and the whole pile would shift. The ash also makes the wood difficult to cut. You would have to sharpen your chainsaw every hour."

The Army Corps of Engineers began dredging the clogged rivers. The mud flow had made the Toutle and Cowlitz riverbeds a fraction of their former size, and that made them likely to flood. To enlarge the riverbeds, the Corps dragged 25 million cubic yards (19 million cu m) of mud out of the banks. But even when the job was finished, the riverbeds were smaller than they used to be and the local residents prepared for floods.

The Columbia River had to be dredged, too. The eruption had thrown a shoal across the river which closed Portland to large cargo ships. This was a desperate situation, since one out of eight jobs in the Portland area depend on the port. By August, however, the river was dredged and the port was open.

There was no doubt that the eruption of Mount St. Helens hurt the tourist business in the state of Washington. The town of Cougar is an example. Normally, the town is filled with tourists in the summer. But the summer of 1980 was different.

Washington State had blocked the roads in a 20-mile (32-km) circle around Mount St. Helens to keep people out of an area called the Red Zone. Cougar was inside the Red Zone.

One of the residents described the situation: "We call Cougar 'East Berlin, USA' because they put the roadblock up on us. We had to sign our rights away to get a permit to come in here. I mean it. It was almost like

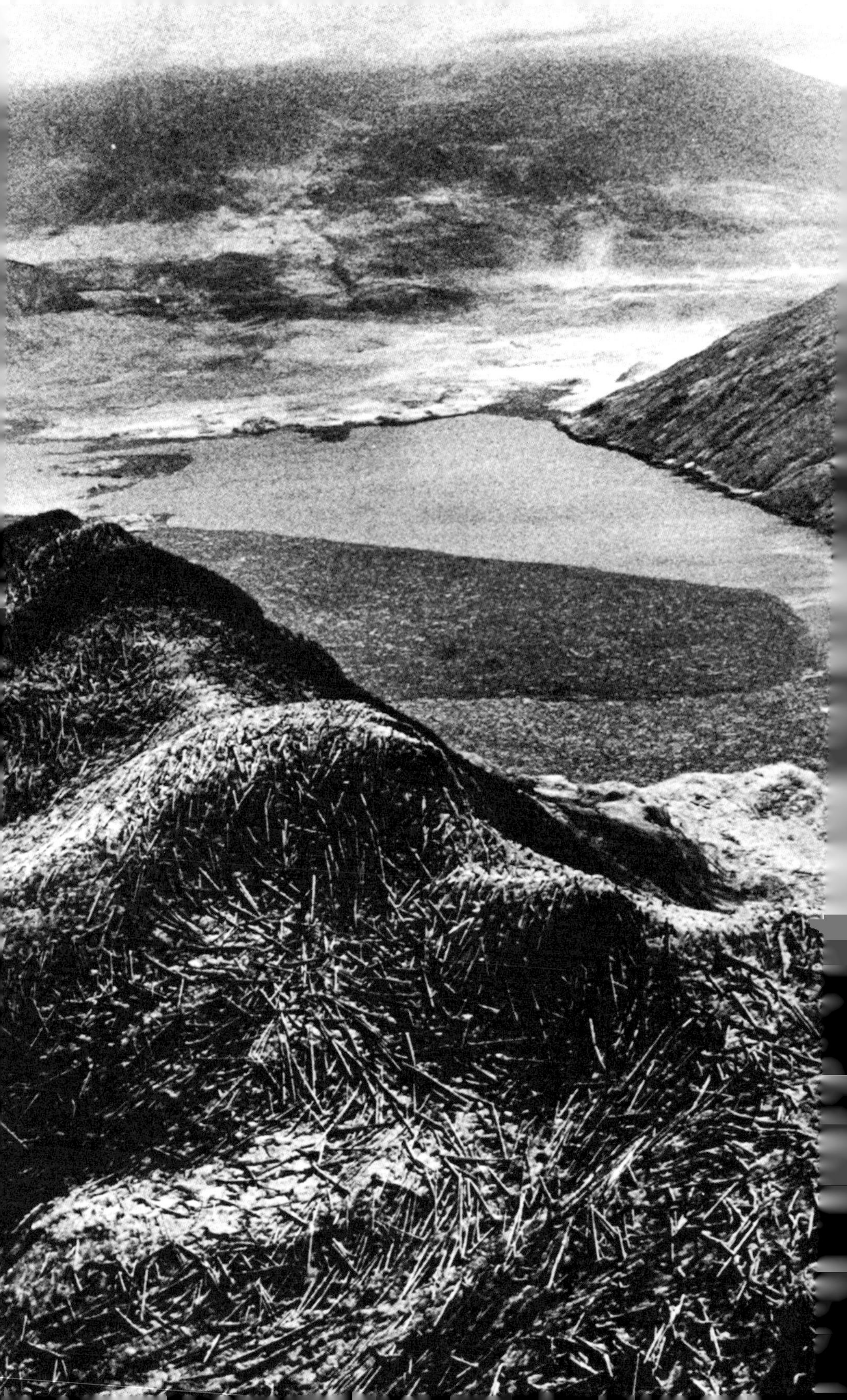

living in a communist country because they dictated to you what you could and could not do. Who can come in and who can't. And some of the papers have referred to the rope-off as the Berlin Wall."

The roadblock stood until October.

Portland, Oregon, was even harder hit, although it is 50 miles (80 km) from Mount St. Helens. The tourist business fell off considerably. A computer firm decided to cancel its plans to build assembly plants in the area. Computers must be assembled in a pollution-free atmosphere, and company officials thought that the problem of pollution would be too big to solve.

The families of the victims who had been buried under tons of mud, rocks, and superheated volcanic ash were confronted with legal problems. Washington law said that their estates could not be admitted to probate, because missing persons were not presumed dead until seven years had passed. Of course, this was not a problem for the families of the other victims, those whose bodies had been recovered.

Robert K. Leick, the prosecuting attorney and coroner of Skamia County, where Mount St. Helens is located, solved the problem. One large hearing on all the missing persons was held. Afterward he ruled that all of the missing people were legally dead. "The insurance companies accepted those findings," he said. "Social Security accepted them. We didn't have any problem at all. We went to the legislature. We got the law changed to allow us to sign presumptive death certificates where we didn't have a body, for people who are presumed killed in the event of a disaster."

One month after the explosion, mud, debris, and blasted timber surrounded Spirit Lake.

Governor Ray had a legal problem, too. In May 1981, she was named in a civil suit filed by the families of eight of the people who died in the eruption. They claimed that the state should have declared more of the area off limits to the public when Mount St. Helens first began to rumble.

CHAPTER SEVEN

SCIENTISTS AND VOLCANOES

The weather is to blame for most kinds of natural disasters. And every one of us has experienced at least one of what are called meteorological disasters—hurricanes, typhoons, thunderstorms, floods, and the like. But there are two other kinds of natural disasters that are caused by forces under the earth's surface. These geological disasters are earthquakes and volcanic eruptions. And there is a connection between the two.

Some of the most earthquake-prone areas of the globe are near volcanoes, and when a volcano erupts, you almost always find that the eruption is accompanied by earthquakes.

To understand the connection between the two, we have to know a little bit about the structure of the earth. There is a crust surrounding the earth that consists of two kinds of rocks. Forming the greater part of the floor of the oceans is a type of rock called *sima*, which is dense and heavy and carries a great deal of the metal magnesium. Forming most of the land areas is a type of rock called *sial*, which is lighter and carries a great deal of the metal aluminum.

Consider that the continents on the earth are like beds of sial that "float" on a layer of sima. Consider also that the continental blocks stick down deeply into the sima. That means that just a small amount of their volume is seen above the surface.

Now take a look at a map of the world. You can see that if the continents of Europe and Africa were shoved westward to the shores of the continents of North and South America, they would fit together somewhat like pieces in a jigsaw puzzle. This landmass would look like a huge supercontinent.

It has been said that the first person to notice this was the English philosopher Francis Bacon, in 1620. But no one paid any attention to the idea. In 1858, an American, Antonio Snider, suggested that there was once such a supercontinent that broke up during the Biblical flood.

It wasn't until 1912 that a serious scientist came up with a theory explaining how the continents had split up. Alfred Wegener, a German meteorologist, astronomer, and geophysicist, that year proposed the "Continental Drift" theory. He believed that the Old World and the New World were once joined together and began separating about two hundred million years ago.

There were several reasons for his belief. Many plants and animals are very similar on continents that today are thousands of miles apart. Also, the same kinds of rocks can be found in both continents. With the appropriate fit, old rocks in South America would lie next to old rocks in Africa, for example, and young rocks would meet other young rocks. Coal beds and fossil remains would also match up.

It was suggested that the continents actually drifted like icebergs on the surface of the earth. Those who agreed with Wegener hypothesized that there once was a gigantic landmass (they named it Gondwanaland) made of what is today South America, India, Australia, and Antarctica. A second landmass (they called it Laurasia) was made of today's North America and Europe.

Wegener's idea created an uproar. One reason was that at the time there was no way of explaining how these landmasses broke up to form the modern continents. It was hard to imagine a force so strong that it could move continents. After all, the smallest continent, Australia, weighs 550 trillion tons.

Another problem that Wegener had was that he did not have the respect of other scientists. He was an outsider, an astronomer who had turned to meteorology as his main work, and thus they considered him an amateur. The debate went on for more than fifty years.

New evidence to support the Continental Drift theory was reported in the mid-1960s. Dr. J. Tuzo Wilson of the University of Toronto pointed out that there is an undersea mountain range that runs through the Atlantic Ocean, and there is a trough, or valley, that runs down the middle of this range. Heat currents from deep within the earth emerge from this trough. Wilson suggested that these currents could have provided the energy to force the continents apart. And rock specimens from the trough are thirty times younger than rocks on the continents.

Wilson went on to suggest that the Indian Ocean was formed by the separation of Africa, India, Australia, and Antarctica. This was supported by Australian scientists who estimated that their continent is 3,400 miles (5,470 km) farther from North America than it was one hundred million years ago. Australia, it was calculated, seems to be drifting at a rate of 2 inches (5.1 cm) per year.

Scientists continued to argue for most of the 1960s. Dr. H. W. Menard of the Scripps Institute of Oceanography in La Jolla, California, pointed out that the ocean bottom geography of the Atlantic and the Pacific were different. Therefore, if the heat currents forced the Old and New Worlds apart, shouldn't the ocean bottoms be similar?

PLATE ACTIVITY

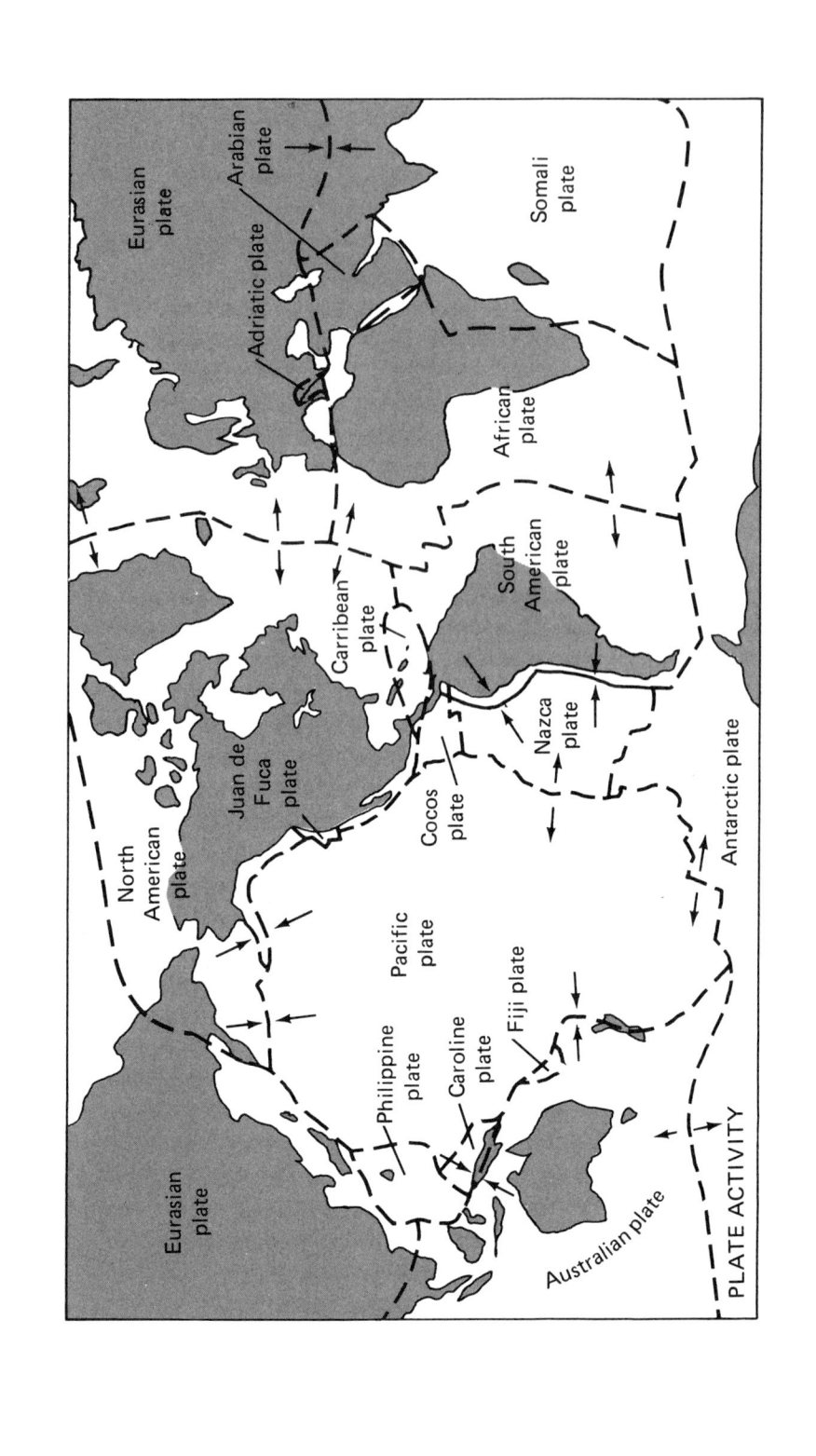

Finally, in the late 1960s computers seemed to have solved the problem. They were able to map the edges of the continents (which are below sea level) and discover some good fits between South America and West Africa, and between other landmasses.

It was also suggested that the drifting of the landmasses was caused by *convection currents*. A convection current has a circulatory movement caused by a transfer of heat. Imagine a room being heated by a radiator. The air is warmed by the radiator and rises. It becomes cooler as it rises, and then descends, is heated again, rises again, and so on, in a circulatory motion. In the case of the drifting landmasses, water is heated by radioactive heat from under the surface of the earth; it rises as the cooler water descends, is heated, then rises again.

When these oceanic convection currents start, the continent can be split by a *rift*, or gap. The depth of the rift may be as much as 100 miles (160 km). Rocks at that depth are very hot and are carried upward through the sial and sima and widen the gap. As they rise up they build a ridge on the ocean floor. This compresses the sial and sima and pushes them farther from the edge of the rift.

This idea, when combined with Wegener's theory, created a new science that was called *plate tectonics*. It is now believed that the outer layer of the earth is made up of about twelve huge plates of rock that are constantly drifting. The cracks, or *fissures*, between these plates form a network all over the earth's surface and the oceans' floors.

Suppose that magma, or molten liquid rock, is forced upward through these fissures in the sea floor. The pressure of this welling up would cause the sea floor to spread. It is known that the two plates in the Pacific Ocean are moving away from each other, pushing the leading edges of the ocean floor against the surrounding continents. The sea floor is being forced underneath the continents into the earth's molten mantle (the interior part of the earth lying between the solid core and the crust).

The stresses of this process could cause both earthquake and volcanic activity. And the Pacific Ocean is a hotbed of volcanoes and earthquakes. Eighty percent of the earthquake and volcanic energy released in the world is found around the edge of this ocean. This circular zone of volcanoes, called the *Ring of Fire,* includes Mount St. Helens.

Most of the remainder of earthquake and volcanic energy is given off along the Mid-Atlantic Ridge, where the North American and Eurasian plates are pulling apart, and along a belt that stretches across the Mediterranean, the Middle East, and India, connecting with the Circum-Pacific Belt from Japan to the Philippines.

So most earthquakes and volcanic eruptions are caused by inner strains deep in the earth. Earthquakes occur when two plates rub roughly past one another. But what causes volcanic eruptions?

When the leading edge of one plate is forced down under the edge of another plate, the rocks of the first plate are subjected to intense heat. This heat comes from the center of the earth and the radioactivity of the surrounding rock. Sometimes this solid rock on the plate melts and forms magma. The magma, lighter than the surrounding rock, is forced upward. Thus, when plates collide or ride up on each other, volcanoes occur on the overriding edge.

There are two categories of volcanoes. Mount St. Helens is an example of what is called the *strato,* or *composite,* type. The cone of the volcano is steep and symmetrical. Strato volcanic eruptions can be dangerous, because the eruptions tend to be explosive, blowing up like a bomb blast.

The *shield* type of volcano has gently sloping sides

January 1980

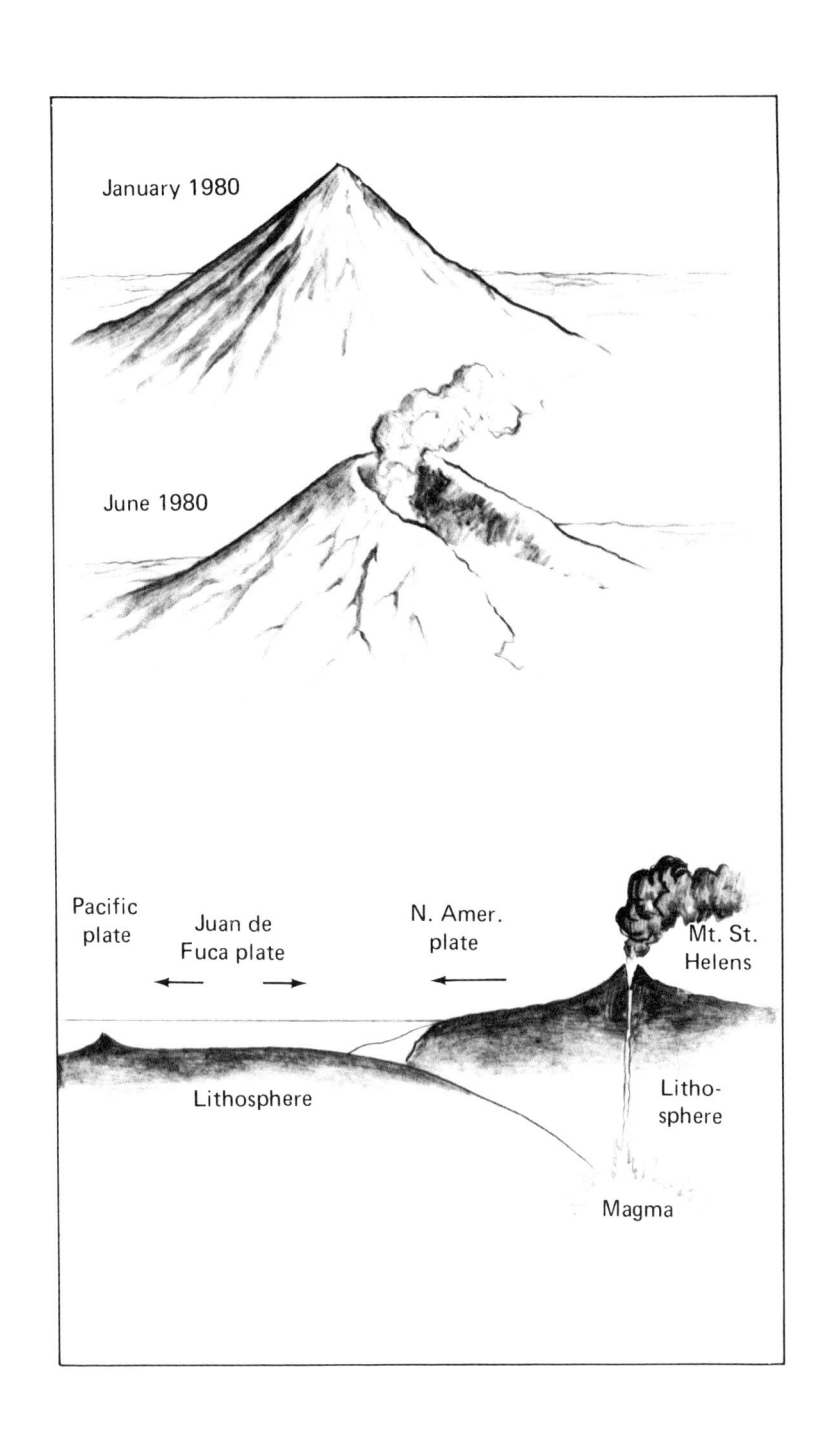

June 1980

Pacific plate

Juan de Fuca plate

N. Amer. plate

Mt. St. Helens

Lithosphere

Lithosphere

Magma

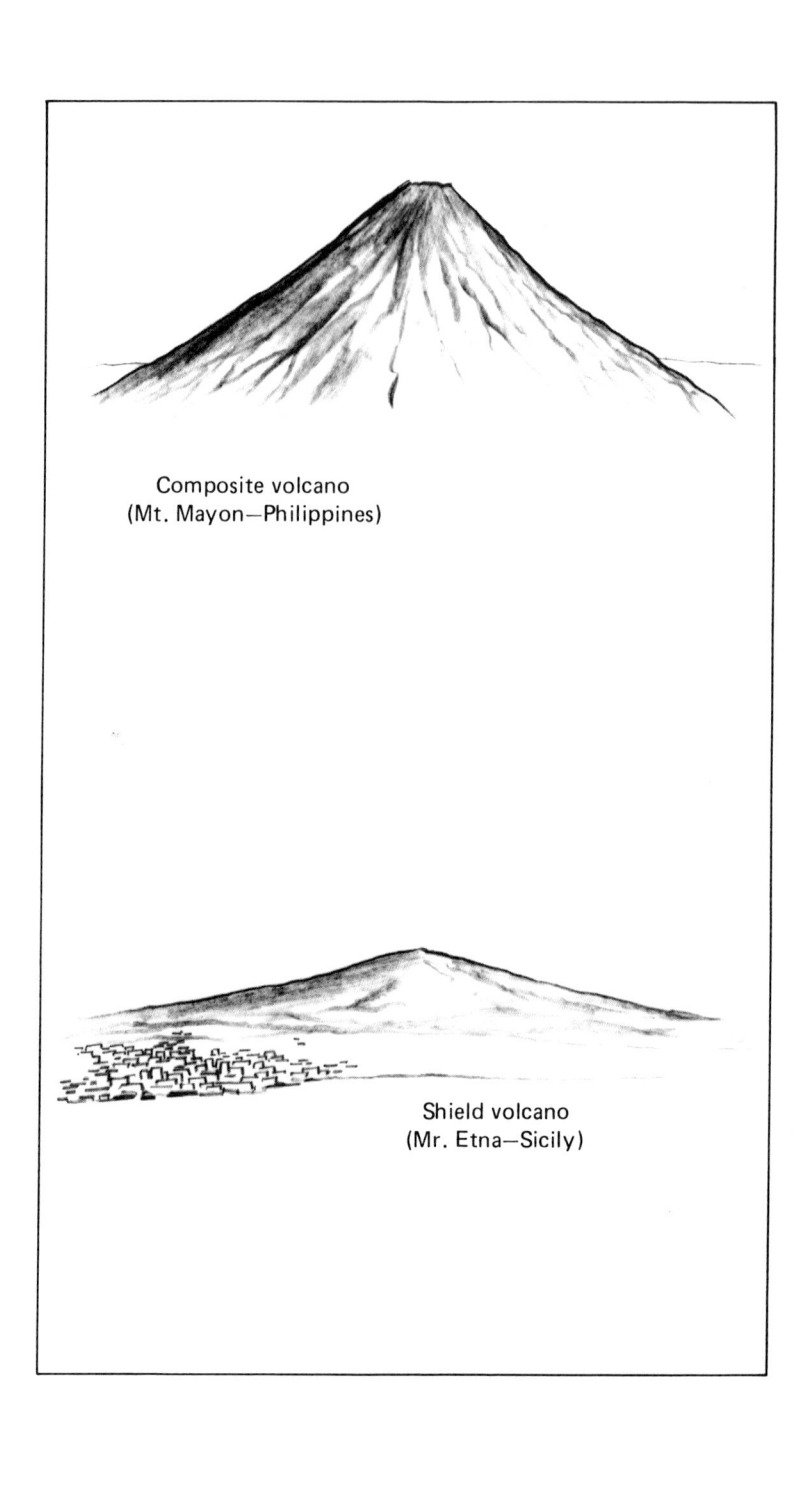

Composite volcano
(Mt. Mayon—Philippines)

Shield volcano
(Mr. Etna—Sicily)

and is usually found on midocean islands, such as Iceland or Hawaii. Its eruptions are less explosive, and they tend to ooze quickly flowing lava.

Another method of classifying volcanoes is by their types of eruptions. Most geologists list five types, although there are those who hold out for six.

Hawaiian volcanoes are the gentlest and send out steady but slow eruptions of runny, fluid lava. This free-flowing material allows any trapped gases to bubble off easily. There is no chance of a violent explosion because no gas gets trapped long enough for the buildup to force the volcano to blow its top.

Strombolian volcanoes, named for the volcano which forms an island between Italy and Sicily, erupt thicker lava. In this case, the gas can build up and burst out in small explosions every few minutes, shooting lumps of half-molten lava into the air. Strombolian volcanoes are more noisy than dangerous.

Vulcanian volcanoes, named for Vulcano, a volcano in Sicily, may erupt for months, blasting solid blocks of material clear of the crater. They produce great quantities of ash, which are spread by volcanic gas in a great plume, like smoke from a huge chimney. They may also produce an outflow of lava.

Vesuvian volcanoes, named after Mount Vesuvius, near Naples, Italy, produce a more persistent plume of gas and ash which forces its way higher up into the atmosphere. Since this is so, it may be safer than the Vulcanian volcano, because the ash is carried up far enough that it disperses before it hits the ground.

Plinian volcanoes, named after the Roman scholar Pliny the Elder, who died in the eruption of Mount Vesuvius in A.D. 79, eject an amount of material that is mind-boggling. In the eruption of Vesuvius, it is estimated that Pompeii, 5 miles (8 km) away, was covered by 9 feet (2.7 m) of volcanic debris. Vesuvius shot out 1 cubic mile (2.6 cu km) of material in forty-eight hours.

In volcanic eruptions the smaller fragments of material can form a type of avalanche that sweeps out from the volcano to engulf anything in its path. The most terrible of these kinds of avalanches, and the type that Mount St. Helens spawned, is a glowing avalanche of gas and molten lava called the *nuée ardente*. It is a violently active hot avalanche in which solid material is suspended in a wall of advancing gas. Supported and swept along in this way, the ash can cover a very great distance in a very short time. There is seldom a warning before a nuée ardente. And when it occurs, all living things in its path are killed by the heat.

Another, more common hazard of volcanic eruptions is the *pyroclastic fall*, which was also present in the Mount St. Helens eruption. Blasts of gas blow bubbling magma out of the volcano, and this magma solidifies into *pumice*, a volcanic glass which contains many small bubbles. Because of the bubbles, pumice is extremely light, so it can be carried over long distances by the wind.

Quite a bit of property damage can be caused by pyroclastic falls, but few living things are usually killed by them. That is, unless the fall is heavy—3½ feet (1 m) or more. This would kill most plants and also would crush flat-roofed houses. Hot fragments from pyroclastic falls have been known to set fire to forests and buildings and cause severe burns and even death.

Pyroclastic flows are devastating, and are another real hazard during an eruption. There are three types, and the first travels with the speed of an atomic blast. It contains low-density, very hot combinations of rock particles and gas flows, and its velocity may hit 100 miles (160 km) per hour.

Small-scale pyroclastic flows have a higher density. They tend to follow the low spots of the surface of the earth. But, being extremely hot, they are just as destructive as the first type.

The third type of pyroclastic flow produces *ignimbrite*. This is a welded glassy ash that looks something like solidified lava. These flows have been known to cover hundreds of square miles to depths of several feet.

Another hazard is the *lava flow*. It is a flow of a large volume of magma that pours out of deep fissures in the cone of the volcano.When the flow is very heavy, it is called a flood eruption, and can do a great deal of damage. Lava flows are not as dangerous as the previously mentioned hazards because they can be diverted into an area where they will cause less damage.

Sometimes a lava flow can be stopped. The flow has a crust on top which keeps the heat in. That means that the lower levels of lava stay hot and liquid and continue to flow. But if the crust can be penetrated, sometimes the lower levels of lava will cool and solidify. Bombs have been used effectively to do just that.

Mudflows are also hazardous. They are often caused by heavy rainstorms during an eruption. Sometimes they have been known to travel at such speeds that they have crushed anything in their paths.

Poisonous gases can be emitted from the volcano. And *tsunamis* (giant ocean waves—commonly called "tidal waves"—triggered by the movement of the earth under a volcano) are other hazards.

Despite their dangers, volcanoes are said to be responsible for the air we breathe and the water we drink. Volcanic vents called *fumaroles* release vast amounts of nitrogen, hydrogen, and carbon dioxide, which are the basic ingredients in the earth's atmosphere. Volcanoes produce water by combining hydrogen and oxygen in their furnaces and ejecting the gas as steam. In addition, much underground water is released through volcanic activity.

Volcanoes in isolated areas pose little threat to human populations. But those in populated areas can cause enormous destruction and death. An example is Mount St. Helens.

What sort of equipment is used by volcanologists? They often use *seismometers*, which are instruments that detect earth tremors. Seismometers are planted in the area around a volcano to record earthquake action which may warn of an approaching eruption.

Tiltmeters are also used. These devices can detect swellings or deflations in the earth's crust or on the side of a volcano. When and if a volcano swells up, its slopes change a bit, and that may mean an upcoming eruption. The tiltmeters have two bulbs with liquid in them. These bulbs are connected to each other by a hollow stem. Liquid flows from one bulb to the other when the slope of the land changes. They are so delicate that a change of a fraction of a degree can be detected.

Lasers are becoming common equipment in the detection of coming eruptions. The laser gun is used to measure a widening or shrinking of a volcano's crater. If it is widening, it could mean an eruption.

Changes in the amount and the temperature of gases coming out of vents on the sides of volcanoes are also measured. An increase in heat or change in composition of the gases may mean an eruption in the future, as can a change in the magnetic and electrical fields of the volcano.

But even with all this equipment and all these measurements, it is still almost impossible to predict an upcoming eruption. Dr. Gordon P. Eaton of the USGS's Hawaiian Volcano Observatory explained: "We don't have a theoretical model for predictions. We are more like social scientists. They see that people usually behave in a certain way and make predictions accordingly, but sometimes people act differently. That's the way it is in studying and predicting volcanoes."

Volcanologists, however, by studying deposits of past eruptions and activities around a certain volcano, can predict an eruption to some degree. But this is only a rough guide to future occurrences. Of course, there are those volcanoes that erupt so regularly that the next eruption can be calculated. But those volcanoes are rare.

Still, more and more data are being gathered. Volcanoes in Alaska, Hawaii, Washington State, California, Guatemala, El Salvador, and Nicaragua have been studied with seismometers and tiltmeters that operate automatically. The data from these instruments are then relayed to a satellite and beamed to a USGS center in Menlo Park, California.

And that is not all. Scientists using several types of approaches, using evidence from the history of the volcano, geological findings, seismic readings, surface tilting, geochemistry, and magnetic and electrical monitoring are working in a variety of places. Among these places are Asama, Japan; Taal, the Philippines; and Bezymianny, in the Soviet Union.

Volcanologists can also be alerted by satellites that have been equipped with infrared scanners. These scanners keep track of ground temperatures and are capable of sensing when a volcano is heating up.

While volcanoes may seem to be a relatively infrequent danger, scientists must continue to study their causes, effects, control, and prediction. The big problem with that is that their best knowledge is often gained only after an eruption, and that was the case with Mount St. Helens.

CHAPTER EIGHT

VOLCANOLOGY AND MOUNT ST. HELENS

After the major eruption in 1980, Mount St. Helens became a "living laboratory" for scientists. And they made full use of it.

It is almost impossible to pinpoint the exact time when certain scientific findings were realized, because discoveries are made over a period of time. But volcanologists did amass a remarkable amount of new data about volcanoes and their actions. And most importantly, this new information enabled them accurately to predict two weeks in advance an eruption of Mount St. Helens that occurred on April 10, 1981. It was a first in volcanology.

After the May 18 eruption, Mount St. Helens was closely monitored. The volcano is located only a few miles from some of the most sophisticated laboratories and research facilities in the world. Scientists everywhere in the country had access, via the United States telecommunications network, to the data that was gathered on the West Coast.

During the week of March 22-28, 1981, almost one year after the major eruption, Christopher Newhall, the USGS hazards coordinator in Vancouver, Washington, reported that deformation in and around the crater had

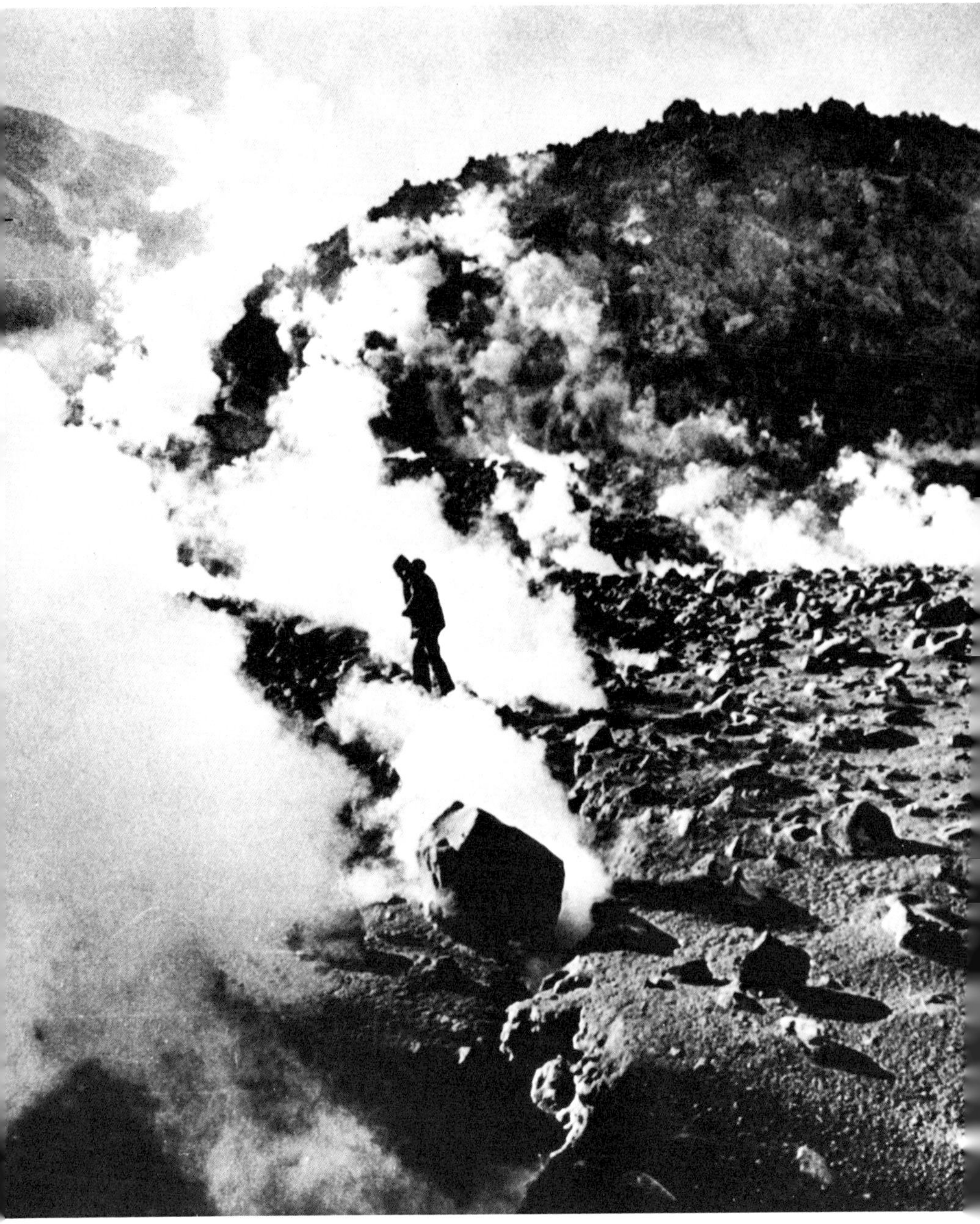

started speeding up. The ground was swelling and another eruption might be on the way. The most precise measurements came from the laser-reflector system on the shore of Spirit Lake, 5 miles (8 km) north of the crater. The reflectors used were of various types—from simple highway reflectors set on poles to sophisticated spectrum prisms. Setting up the reflectors had been dangerous, because the dome could have exploded at any time.

In a laser-reflector system, a laser light is aimed at reflectors placed at various sites in and around the crater. The time it takes for the laser light beam to be reflected back is recorded automatically. This time interval tells scientists the distance between the reflector and the laser light to a fraction of an inch. A change in the time interval means a change in the distance, and, of course, that the crater is swelling.

Tiltmeters recorded every tiny change in the slope of the mountain. Newhall commented on the change in Mount St. Helens' tilt. "Normally, it's a small change, about half a centimeter [.2 inch] per day. That week, the rate increased to as much as a centimeter [.4 inch] per day."

Later, measurements inside the crater showed that the lava dome was swelling upward. About 80 yards (73 m) from the dome, the ground was rising ten times more rapidly than it was half a mile (.8 km) away. There were cracks forming inside the crater, radiating outward from

Exploring the floor of Mount St. Helens' crater, about 75 yards (58 m) from the expanding 45-story lava dome, in February 1981.

the dome across the crater floor. They ranged from a few inches to several yards wide, and they were broadening about .4 inch (1 cm) per day.

Then too, there was movement along the faults in the crater floor. The lava dome appeared to be moving upward and outward over the floor of the crater.

These activities increased during the week of March 22 to 28. On March 28, clouds moved in and scientists had to ground the helicopters and could not reach the crater.

The USGS issued an extended outlook advisory asking people to be on the alert on March 30. Activity under the mountain was increasing, it stated, and an eruption within the next week or two was likely. However, it was too soon to forecast the date or probable nature of such an eruption.

Before that March 1981 prediction, eruption warnings had been vague. They usually had stated something like: "There will be an eruption somewhere in the Pacific Northwest within the next one hundred years." Others had been short-range forecasts made but a few hours before the eruption.

Previously, warnings had been based on seismicity—patterns of quake activity under the mountain. One scientist claimed that that was like an auto mechanic trying to figure out when an engine would fail just by listening to the engine's noise. This time, other instruments, such as lasers and surveying equipment, were used in conjunction with seismic devices.

Tiltmeters began to show that the south face of the mountain was getting steeper slopes as the mountain inflated. Then the mountain deflated. Some scientists thought this meant that a rising blob of magma inflated the lower slopes and then passed upward, deflating the slopes. Other scientists speculated that Mount St. Helens contained a long tube that was sucking up molten rock.

Then came the April 10 explosion. Modern communications and transportation could not cope. A DC-9 flew through the ash cloud and damaged its engines. The Air Force and Army had to fly aircraft away from McCord Air Force Base and Fort Lewis in the state of Washington.

Eleven hundred miles (1,770 km) of Washington roads were impassable. Ten thousand motorists were stranded. Police vehicles were stalled by ash-clogged air filters and fuel lines. Train service was halted. Shipping channels were clogged by timber and mud in the Cowlitz and Columbia Rivers. Ash particles in the sky produced lightning that knocked out power lines.

A McDonnell Douglas B-23 was sent up by the University of Washington to gather particle size and gas abundance data. Then "in a fit of insanity," as the pilot later described his actions, he attempted to fly into the plume. He abandoned this quickly when the aircraft was peppered with volcanic debris the size of baseballs.

Other research planes trailing hoses that sucked in gas flew into the plume. Inside the planes were instruments to measure carbon dioxide and sulfur dioxide. Those gases were coming out of the mountain's vent at rates of up to 16,000 tons per day.

Survey teams went out into the ash-smothered area to make a contour map of ash thickness. They discovered that the ashfall totaled 150 million tons.

After the eruption, scientists went back into the crater. Bernard Chouet, a research associate in the Department of Earth and Planetary Science at the Massachusetts Institute of Technology, described his work: "It's actually pretty cold in the crater." The high altitude, Chouet explained, makes the air at the summit feel wintry even on a warm spring day. At the same time, heat from very energetic steam vents, or fumaroles, in the crater floor give off intense warmth to anybody standing nearby. The effect is rather like sitting in front of an old-fashioned kitchen stove on a winter night: you feel hot in front and cold in back. Chouet added that there were scores of vents and some of them were "clearly glowing red."

It is thought that the presence or lack of a dome may be important in the prediction of a volcanic eruption. It seems that when there is a dome, earthquakes close to the surface increase in frequency before the eruption. If there isn't a dome, magma and gases can flow and cause harmonic tremors. These are continuous low-level movements in the earth. As the power of these eruptions increases, so does the chance of an eruption.

Scientists also learned about the dangers of air-blast explosions, like the one that sheared away the north flank of Mount St. Helens on May 18. Dr. Robert Yeats, the chairman of the Geology Department at Oregon State University, remarked, "Before May 18 we had known almost nothing about air-blast explosions and their products. We know a great deal more about them now, in terms of hazards to people. Until then, we were talking primarily about people getting killed by mudflows and by pyroclastic flows, but not by air blast, which accounted for most of the loss of life."

Steve Malone, a volcano expert, said, "More accomplishments are yet to come, because the data are still being worked on. That's the exciting thing. This is a fantastic natural laboratory. It will give us a lot of new insights into processes going on in volcanoes, and that will have practical implications for reducing hazards both here in the United States and around the world."

A symposium on Mount St. Helens was held at Oregon State University one year to the day after the first jet of ash and steam came out of the volcano, on March 27, 1980. USGS hazards coordinator Newhall observed at the meeting that "there seem to be crude correlations between earth tides and eruptions. But for some volcanoes there is no correlation. I think whether or not a volcano erupts on the high tide depends on whether it is set to erupt already—a hair-trigger situation. The tide could not make it erupt if it weren't set to do so. But our laboratory is at nature's discretion. We have much less control over the experiments we can conduct."

Donald Peterson, the scientist in charge of studies of the mountain for the USGS reflected: "Volcanology is a strange science. It's a hybrid, made up of a combination of geology, chemistry, physics—a whole host of specialized versions of each one of these. We're using the most modern techniques of all these sciences and turning them toward problems of volcanoes, which are very complex physical, chemical, and geological phenomena. There's an element of luck involved that laboratory science doesn't necessarily have."

At the symposium, scientists reported clues that helped them track the series of events during the May 18 eruption, including precisely timed seismic records and photographs taken by both scientists and visitors to the area. They felt that what had started the whole eruption on May 18 was a rather severe earthquake that measured 5 on the Richter Scale. The quake blew out the bulge on the north face, which caused the enormous landslide—the largest one ever recorded. The bulge slid down the mountain, and one scientist compared it to a "vast sliding door." The new opening in the mountain allowed gas to escape with such force that it threw huge rocks toward the north.

Across the Pacific in Kamchatka, in the Soviet Union, a sister volcano, Mount Bezymianny, erupted in 1955 in the same way. Its side blew out and the end product was mudslides all over the surrounding valley. Later, as it had happened with Mount St. Helens, a dome grew inside the crater. And Bezymianny has erupted several times since 1955.

Taking his clue from the Soviet volcano, Dr. Stephen D. Malone, a seismologist at the University of Washington, thinks that Mount St. Helens may continue to erupt for perhaps twenty more years.

Peterson added that the most useful information that could be used in prediction came from seismic tremors. Also, the dome's growth during eruptions was useful. The growth had been measured by laser instruments, and the main site for laser installations had been Harry's Ridge, named for Harry R. Truman.

The laser measurements indicated that the crater floor had been pushed outward by the swelling of the dome. The north side of the crater had been pushed to the north some 47 inches (119 cm) during the five days surrounding the December 25 eruption in 1980.

Tiltmeters had been installed at three places on the volcano, but they could not be used in the most active areas. They would have been overrun by lava, and a tiltmeter costs about $2,000.

It was also pointed out that Mount St. Helens' lava is rich in silica, a compound found in sand, quartz, and opal. The silica thickened the lava and made it stiff, and the result was that the lava clogged the volcano vents. That, in turn, caused enormous gas pressure to build up inside the volcano. This buildup of pressure might have caused the explosion.

After the April 1980 eruption, it was found that the silica content of the Mount St. Helens lava was diminishing. So it was thought that more explosions were unlikely. That hope turned out to be groundless.

Scientists also found hydrogen gas escaping from the crater floor. It seemed to have been released from the molten rock as it solidified. They came to the conclusion that escaping hydrogen also might be a predictor of an upcoming explosion.

Those scientists hoping to study the connection between volcanoes and climate were disappointed with the Mount St. Helens eruption. They had expected it to influence the world's weather. However, it didn't thicken the haze in the stratosphere enough, it didn't block out enough sunlight, and it didn't cool the area near the ground enough to have an impact on the climate.

Apparently the eruption had produced only a small amount of sulfurous gases. These gases, converted to droplets of sulfuric acid in the stratosphere, block sunlight and so cool the lower atmosphere. In the past, such a cooling of the atmosphere has lasted a few years after an eruption, and this had affected the weather for decades.

Some scientists disagree with the sulfuric acid theory. It is hard to prove, but the study of glaciers has produced new evidence. The deep ice cores from glaciers were removed to find the amount of sulfuric acid in the ice. Ice is laid down in glaciers in layers, and the age of a particular layer can be calculated.

The age can be dated back to A.D. 553 with only a one-to-three-year certainty. The major known eruptions would have caused the ice formed in those years to have a greater amount of sulfuric acid in it. In between eruptions, the acidity varied from year to year.

The 1815 eruption of Tambora in Indonesia was supposed to have caused what became known as "the year without a summer." In Central Greenland, the ice formed that year had an estimated 150 million tons of acid in it. But the Danish scientists who took these measurements, C. U. Hammer, H. B. Clausen, and Willi Dansgaard of the University of Copenhagen, pointed out in 1981 that the acid is not always perfectly preserved in the ice. Soil dust with carbonate minerals could have neutralized all or part of it. Then there is the problem that tiny nearby eruptions would deposit as much acid as massive ones farther away.

When will Mount St. Helens erupt next and in what direction will the ash go? Geologists can't answer that. They know the volcano's history but not its future plans.

Mike Folsom of Eastern Washington University explained: "There is what's called the Pacific Ring of Fire. And the Cascade Mountain Range is a part of that—only a very small part of it. We have reason to believe that the Cascades will be geologically, if not volcanically, active for a long time. There's a great deal of geothermal heat being made available from Mount Rainier, and there's no reason to believe that Mount Rainier is just going to sit there. It's very likely to become active, and very likely to become very active in our lifetime.

"And if Mount Rainier does become active, there are a number of rather frightening consequences that could occur. One of those is mudflows. About 5,000 years ago there was a large mudflow which flowed 35 miles [56 km] away from the vent of Mount Rainier. It flowed down toward Tacoma and it covered the flats of a portion of Puget Sound in that area with as much as 70 feet [21 m] of very wet rock mud debris.

"It's kind of surprising that nothing has been active recently in the Cascades, with the exception of Mount Lassen in California. Mount Lassen erupted in 1914 and there were almost 150 separate and distinct events during that year. Then it had a summit explosion similar to Mount St. Helens."

Scientists theorize that if one volcano awakens from dormancy, others in the mountain chain will, too. Records indicate that when Mount St. Helens erupted in the past, other volcanoes became active. So the USGS feels that the Cascade volcanoes may be entering a period of heightened activity.

Robert I. Tilling, chief of geochemistry and geophysics at the USGS National Center in Reston, Virginia, commented, "We certainly are not predicting that more Cascade volcanoes are about to erupt. At the same time, these initial stirrings—in the form of earthquake storms and minor steaming—suggest that the Cascade volcanoes may be awakening and could produce activity for the next several decades, possibly including major eruptions."

The coastal volcanoes of the Cascade Range are all connected in their subsurface roots, some 125 miles (200 km) down. Richard Armstrong, a geologist at the University of British Columbia, has warned, "We are in the middle of a period of vigorous volcanic mountain building."

He claimed that fifty million years ago, there was an enormous amount of volcanic activity in British Columbia, which continued for millions of years. As recently as two thousand years ago, huge eruptions of ash occurred, creating regions of absolute desolation with mudflow, river blockings, and ashfalls—similar to what is happening now.

Because of this potential for increased activity, the USGS has accelerated their volcano monitoring, hazards mapping, and risk assessment to help minimize the dangers and impact of possible future eruptions. As part of the stepped-up programs, a field office was set up at Vancouver, Washington for monitoring Mount St. Helens and other Cascade volcanoes, and volcanic hazards assessment reports were issued for Oregon's Mount Hood and California's Mount Shasta.

The 11,235-foot (3,425-m) Mount Hood, 45 miles (72 km) east of Portland, is one of the most carefully watched mountains in the Cascade Range. It last erupted in the mid-1880s, but little historical information is available.

Mount Baker also seems a likely prospect for an eruption. Just south of the Canadian border in Washington, it and Mount St. Helens erupted almost simultaneously in 1843, 1854, and 1857-58. Also, Mount Baker has shown increasing activity in its fumaroles since 1975, leading to the closing of Mount Baker National Park. Mount Rainier, in Washington, which steams periodically, and Mount Lassen, in California, are also active.

CHAPTER NINE

BIOLOGY AND MOUNT ST. HELENS

Immediately after the May 18 eruption, fisheries biologists apprehensively waited for the Chinook salmon to make their annual spring trip up the mud-clogged Cowlitz River. But the biologists discovered that the fish avoided their native river and headed up the nearby Kalama River instead.

Most broadleaf trees did not suffer very extensive damage from the ashfall, because much of their respiration is done through stomata, or tiny holes, on the undersides of the leaves.

After the eruption, there was a sudden exodus of birds in areas of eastern Washington where the ashfall was heavy. The ash had killed the insects that were the chief diet of the birds. Bees, which are essential to fruit production in the Yakima Valley east of the volcano, suffered greatly. The fine ash dusted their wings and made flight impossible.

But by September, deer tracks had been spotted on the barren slopes of Mount St. Helens. Ferns, skunk cabbage, and tree sprouts also appeared. Farmers had a bumper crop of hops because the slight acidity of the ash helped to neutralize the alkaline soil, thus causing the ground to retain the heavy rains of May and June.

In May of 1981, some of the birds had returned. John Patterson, research manager of the Washington Department of Game, said, "As far as game birds are concerned, there were some nest losses, but there was re-nesting. We have no long-term data on nongame species, but we feel, just based on what happened to the game birds, that there was no real impact." He also noted that there was still no permanent wildlife in the immediate vicinity of the volcano because of the almost total lack of greenery there.

Millions of fish and thousands of game animals and furbearers were wiped out. Colonies of at least seven subspecies of bats—including some that were found only near Mount St. Helens—may have disappeared forever. Nearby, an entire herd of mountain goats perished. All the ptarmigan seemed to have been killed. There were predictions that 1.5 million game animals and birds could eventually be lost in the state of Washington alone.

Jay Stockbridge of the Washington Department of Game was not optimistic: "It's not just a question of when Mount St. Helens' animal populations can make a comeback. They can't come back at all if there's no place for them to come back to. These animals were forced into surrounding areas where they had to compete with other animals of their own kind. This resulted in overcrowding and death."

But Jack Shero, Deputy Superintendent of the Washington Department of Natural Resources, was not so gloomy: "We think that eventually we'll have another forest in there—it just depends on how well the new growth takes beneath the ash."

Bill Ruediger, a United States Forest Service biologist, explained the situation: "Ecologically, it's just a regenerative process. Most of the plant communities that were in the area before the blast will re-establish themselves in time, and some new ones that never existed there may also appear. The eruptions created thousands of snag trees. As soon as the woodpeckers begin boring holes in them, there will be some pretty good new habitats for species like the mountain bluebird. So the blasts should eventually help enhance future populations of many creatures."

One negative finding was reported by dairy farmers. Milk production in their herds was down as much as 30 percent. Scientists feared that if the same effect were found in milk production in deer and elk, many of their young would die from starvation. The death toll of young deer and elk has not yet been tabulated.

Then there was the decline in the insect population. Don White, manager of the Turnbull National Wildlife Refuge near Spokane, talked about that. "We normally see a lot of wasps in this area, but I haven't seen one since the blast."

Aquatic insects were particularly hard hit by the high concentrations of nitrates and ammonia in the water. So the source of much food for fish was eliminated.

White also commented about the waterfowl loss. "Our preliminary census of waterfowl breeding looks grim. Right now, we estimate that it is only about 10 percent of normal . . . ." Many adult birds had abandoned their nests, leaving their young to suffocate. The northern spotted owl was classified as "threatened" in Oregon, and the state of Washington considered putting it on the endangered species list.

Ruediger said, "We're very concerned about the owl because it requires large stands of old-growth Douglas fir trees for nesting, and the state's biggest stand of such trees was destroyed by the blast. It will be 250 years for a similar stand to develop."

Twenty percent of the songbird population was wiped out. The eruption destroyed the entire 1979 Chinook and coho salmon brood stock—10.8 million fish in the Toutle River. Sixty-six thousand non-hatchery-reared salmon were also killed. The salmon loss totaled $2.5 million. Four hundred thousand trout and other fish were killed, and their spawning areas were lost.

A year after the first eruption, the landscape was still desolate. The once crystal-blue Coldwater Lake was muddy brown. Spirit Lake was black, smelled of sulfur—just like rotten eggs—and was filled with thousands of dead trees.

But ecologists found flowers on the edge of Spirit Lake. These flowers were those of a hardy rhizome, *Lysichitum americanum*, commonly called skunk cabbage. The flowers represented the return of life to the area.

Patches of green had emerged around Coldwater Lake, growing up among scatterings of bones. The bones, skeletons of elk killed in the blast, were serving as a source of nutrients for the new life.

Other plants were later found on the shores of Spirit Lake—grasslike sedge, horsetail, willow shrubs, miners' lettuce, thistles, henbane, blackberry, lupine, bracken fern, everlasting, and fireweed. Perhaps the most important of those was the henbane, which is a favorite food of deer.

A. B. Adams, a botanist, and his wife, Virginia, a mathematical ecologist, were two of hundreds of scientists who studied the mountain after the eruption. They found eighty-nine different species of plant life, including some seedling conifers.

Much of the area surrounding Mount St. Helens is being studied to learn how nature heals itself after natural disasters.

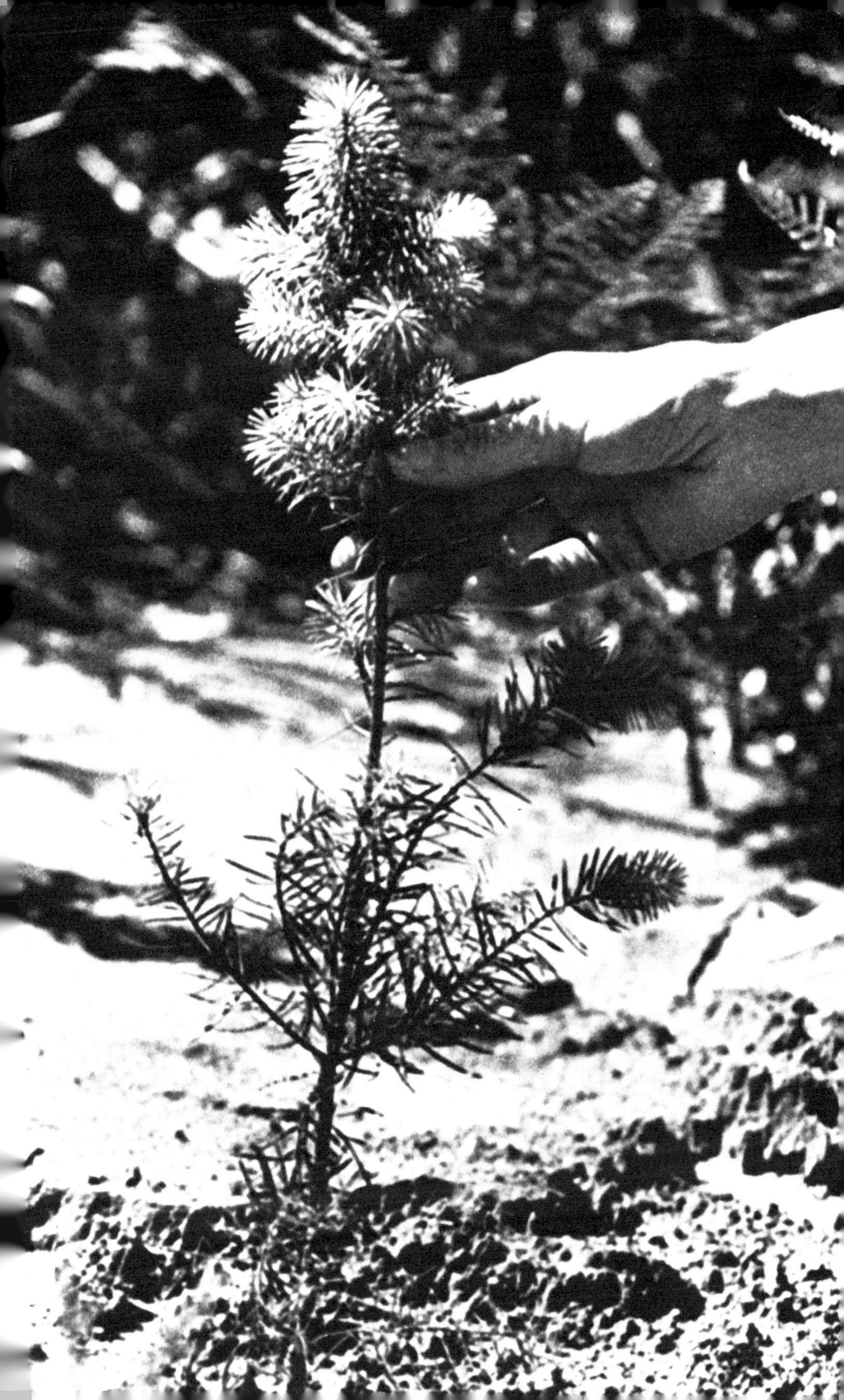

These plants were generally hardy varieties whose root systems, rhizomes, tubers, and bulbs had survived the blast underground and then grew up through the soil and the crust of the ash. This ash crust was rich in potassium and phosphorus, but lacked nitrogen, which is a product of organic decay—the rotting of dead plants and animals. The Adamses also found several insects that were vital to plant pollination. Eventually, there were sightings of elk, deer, coyotes, and other larger animals.

The seemingly dead lakes, laced with sulfur, phenolic acids, tannins, and turpentine from decomposing trees, were found to be filled with microorganisms, such as primitive bacteria. These bacteria were unlike any found in the lakes before the eruption, and seemed to be of quite ancient species, able to draw energy from sulfur and metals deposited in the water by the eruption.

Adams said, "Right at the eruption, you had a primordial system—if you came up here a week afterward, you might have said, 'This must have been the way the earth was—everything steaming and boiling, and, right during the eruption, there might have been lightning. That's why I call it primordial."

The area around Mount St. Helens had, in a sense, gone back to the dawn of time. Everything was starting all over again—but the regeneration might take two hundred years.

CHAPTER TEN

AND AFTER

The story of Mount St. Helens did not end with the beginning of the ecological regeneration. On October 15, 1981, the United States Forest Service announced that almost 85,000 acres (34,400 hectares) of the area would be preserved for public education. Much of the area, most of it to the north of the mountain, would be retained as it was after the eruption, and no rehabilitation would be attempted.

John Johnson, a member of the planning staff for the USFS, explained, "One of the major areas of interest will be to see how nature is healing itself. It will provide a large area for protection of significant geologic and biologic features, while providing for timber salvage and rehabilitation in some of the heavily damaged areas."

The plan permitted calving for elk, and it was thought that the area could support at least 70 percent of the numbers of deer and elk that were there before the explosion.

One grim effect of the eruption was that the ash had hidden the bodies of two young women for a year and a half after they had been murdered. On October 17, 1981, the bodies, each with one gunshot wound, were discovered by pheasant hunters.

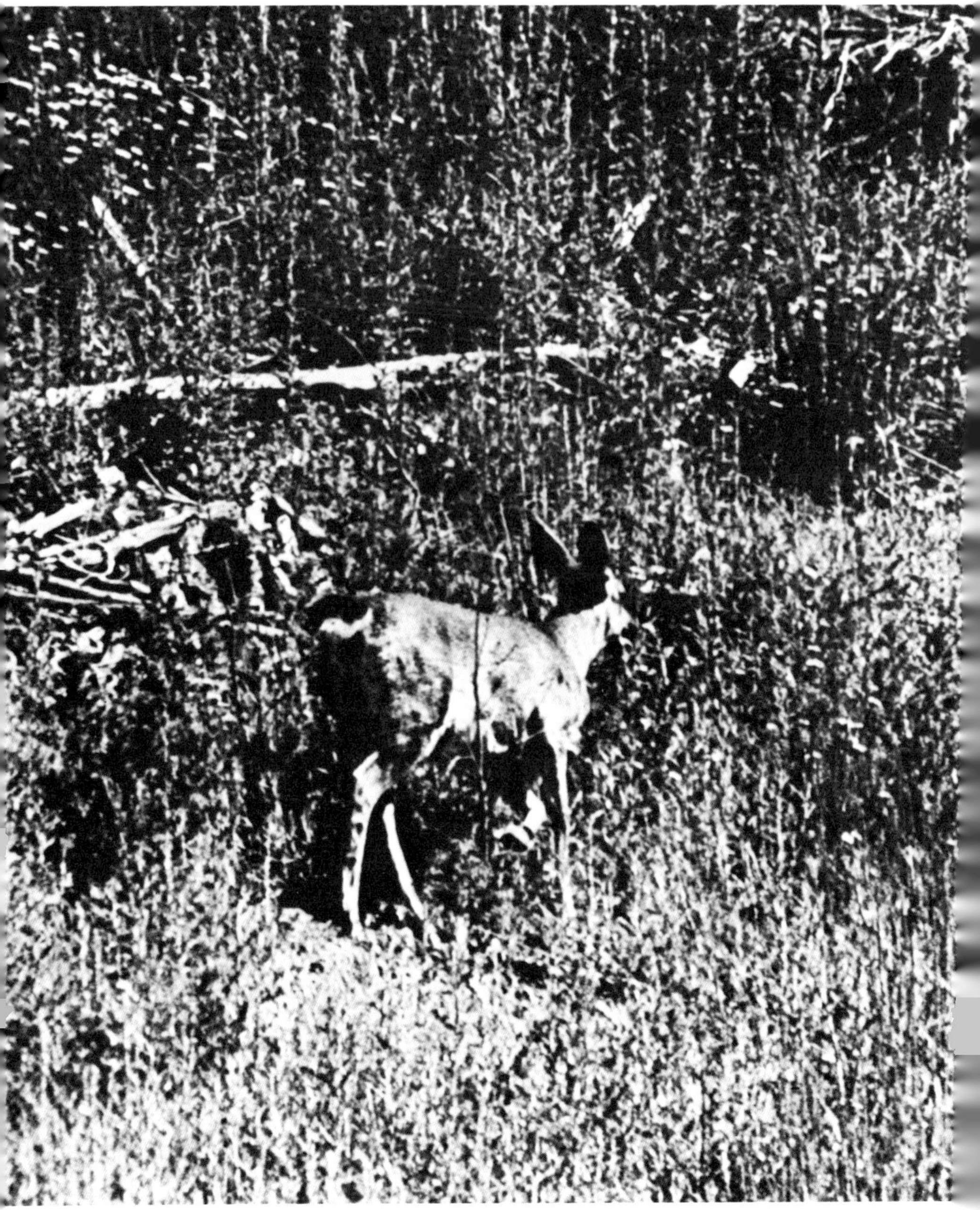

Geologists have predicted that eventually the dome will grow to fill the crater. That might restore Mount St. Helens to its original height. So the story of this awesome and powerful mountain is not over.

Many animals have returned to the National Forest area since the 1980 eruption.

GLOSSARY

Convection current: A current caused by the movement of heated material through a fluid. Colder, denser material causes warmer, less dense material to rise.

Epicenter: The point on the earth's surface directly above the focus of an earthquake.

Friatic eruption: An eruption in which heat rises from deep magma and melts the icy cap of a volcano causing a steam explosion.

Geothermal energy: The heat beneath the surface of the earth.

Ignimbrite: A glassy, welded ash that is the product of a pyroclastic volcano flow.

Lahar: A volcanic mudflow.

Lava: Molten rock that escapes from the earth's interior through the earth's surface.

Lithosphere: The outer part of the solid earth.

Magma: A mass of molten rock materials and dissolved gases beneath the surface of the earth.

Mercalli scale: A method of measuring the kind of damage caused by an earthquake in terms of its effect on humans. This method uses a twelve-point scale of intensity.

Nuée ardente: An extremely hot volcanic eruption of gas and lava that looks like a glowing avalanche.

Plate tectonics: The study of the theory of continental drift, based upon the idea that landmasses are constantly moving at a slow rate of speed.

Pumice: A volcanic glass containing many small bubbles.

Pyroclastic fall: A rain of ash or pumice coming from a volcano.

Richter scale: A measure of the ground motion of earthquakes in terms of their energy.

Rift: A gap in the surface of the earth.

Seismograph: A device used to record the ground motion of an earthquake.

Seismometer: A device used to measure the ground motion of an earthquake.

Shield volcano: A volcano with gently sloping sides that often oozes lava during its eruption.

Sial: Aluminum-bearing rocks that form most of the land areas of the earth.

Sima: Magnesium-bearing rocks that form most of the areas on the ocean floor.

Strato volcano: A volcano with a steep, symmetrical cone that often has explosive eruptions.

Tiltmeter: A device used to measure swellings or deflations in the earth's crust.

BIBLIOGRAPHY

BOOKS

Aylesworth, Thomas G. *Geological Disasters: Earthquakes and Volcanoes.* New York: Franklin Watts, 1979.

Butler, Hal. *Nature at War.* Chicago: Henry Regnery, 1976.

Cohen, Daniel. *How the World Will End.* New York: McGraw-Hill, 1973.

Koenninger, Tom (ed.). *Mount St. Helens Holocaust.* Lubbock, Texas: C. F. Boone Publishers/Barron Publications, 1980.

Maloney, William E. *The Great Disasters.* New York: Grosset & Dunlap, 1976.

Navarra, John Gabriel. *Nature Strikes Back.* Garden City, New York: Doubleday, 1971.

Palmer, Leonard, KOIN-TV Newsroom. *Mt. St. Helens.* Portland, Oregon: Lee Enterprises, 1980.

Riedman, Sara R. *How Wildlife Survives Natural Disasters.* New York: David McKay Company, 1977.

Staffs of *The Daily News*, Longview, Washington, and *The Journal-American*, Bellevue, Washington. *Volcano: The Eruption of Mount St. Helens.* Longview, Washington: Longview Publishing, 1980.

Stemman, Roy. *Atlantis and the Lost Lands.* Garden City, New York: Doubleday, 1976.

Watson, Lyall. *Supernature.* Garden City, New York: Anchor Press/Doubleday, 1973.

MAGAZINE ARTICLES

Bonenko, Allen. "After the Blast," *National Wildlife.* October, 1980.

Chrysler, K.M. "A City that Lives in Shadow of Volcano," *U.S. News and World Report.* June 30, 1980.

Cook, R.J., et.al. "Impact on Agriculture of the Mount St. Helens Eruptions," *Science.* January 2, 1981.

"Decoding the Volcano's Message," *Time.* September 22, 1980.

Gribbin, John. "Do Volcanoes Affect the Climate?" *New Scientist.* January 21, 1982.

Keerdoja, Eileen, and Pamela Abramson. "Dixy Lee Ray Is Still Speaking Out," *Newsweek.* June 8, 1981.

Kerr, Richard A. "Mount St. Helens and a Climate Quandary," *Science.* January 23, 1981.

Lane, Laura. "In Spite of Volcanic Ashfall, Farmers Fight Back," *Farm Journal.* January, 1981.

"A Lasting Pall Over the Northwest," *U.S. News and World Report.* June 23, 1980.

MacMahon, James A. "Mount St. Helens Revisited," *Natural History.* May, 1982.

"Meteorology on Ice," *Science and Children.* March, 1982.

"Mount St. Helens Spurs New Scientific Studies," *Aviation Week and Space Technology.* August 18, 1980.

Pardo, Richard. "Rehabilitating St. Helens," *American Forests.* November, 1980.

Ritchie, David. "A Volcano's Fiery Laboratory," *The New York Times Magazine.* March 7, 1982.

"Science Briefs," *The Science Teacher.* May, 1981, April, 1982.

Simon, Cheryl. "The Great Earth Debate," *Science News*. March 13, 1982.

Steinhart, Peter. "The Earth Heaves, The Sky Falls," *Audubon*. January 19, 1981.

———. "Who Rules the Wasteland?" *Audubon*. January 19, 1981.

"Volcanic Payoff," *Omni*. March, 1981.

NEWSPAPER ARTICLES

"Devastated Volcanic Area to Be Preserved by U.S." *The New York Times*. October 15, 1981.

"Eruptive Phase Slows at Mount St. Helens," *The New York Times*. April 8, 1981.

"Evidence of 1980 Murders Hidden by Volcano," *The New York Times*. October 18, 1981.

"Geologists View Lava Dome at Mount St. Helens," *The New York Times*. April 14, 1982.

King, Wayne. "Amid Ash and Mud, a Speck of Life Rises at Volcano," *The New York Times*. May 17, 1981.

"Lava Dome Growing in Mount St. Helens," *The New York Times*. March 22, 1982.

"Lave Eruption Termed Likely at Volcano in Northwest," *The New York Times*. April 3, 1980.

"Mount St. Helens Continues to Rumble," *The New York Times*. March 16, 1981.

"Mount St. Helens Eruption Eases; Small Plume of Steam Is Emitted," *The New York Times*. September 8, 1981.

"Mount St. Helens Erupts in 'a Whisper,'" *The New York Times*. May 15, 1982.

"Mount St. Helens Erupts, Sending Ash to 15,500 Feet," *The New York Times*. April 11, 1981.

"Mount St. Helens Erupts, Spewing Ash High in the Air," *The New York Times*. March 19, 1982.

"Mount St. Helens Lets Off a Little More of Its Steam," *The Advocate* (Stamford, CT). June 20, 1981.

"Mount St. Helens Rumbling Again," *The Advocate* (Stamford, CT). June 19, 1981.

"New Dome," *The Advocate* (Stamford, CT). June 25, 1981.

"Oregon Now Setting up Volcano Emergency Test," *The Advocate* (Stamford, CT). April 24, 1981.

"Philippines Is Harnessing Power of Volcanoes," *The New York Times.* November 15, 1981.

"Presumed Dead," *The New York Times.* July 5, 1981.

"Scientists Eye Crater," *The Advocate* (Stamford, CT). April 24, 1981.

" 'Silent Spring' Scare," *The New York Times.* May 17, 1981.

"Small Quakes Increasing at Mount St. Helens," *The New York Times.* October 30, 1981.

Sullivan, Walter. "The Latest 'Monster Cloud:' Awesome but Not Dangerous," *The New York Times.* April 27, 1982.

———. "St. Helens: Scientists Report the Cause Is Finally Clear," *The New York Times.* April 28, 1981.

"Two Eruptions on Mount St. Helens Prompt Evacuation and Warnings," *The New York Times.* March 21, 1982.

"Volcano Eruptions Continue," *The Advocate* (Stamford, CT). March 21, 1982.

INDEX

Acid ash, 18
Adams, A. B., 70
Aftermath of eruption, 25-32, 73-76
Air-blast explosions, 60
Animals, effect of eruption on, 14, 34, 67-72, 74
Armstrong, Richard, 65
Ash, 15, 18, 20, 25, 27, 28, 29, 59
Asphyxiation, 25
Avalanches, glowing, 15, 50

Bacon, Francis, 42
Batelle Memorial Institute's Northwest Laboratory, 27
Biology, 67-72
Blowup, 15-24
Buildup to eruption, 7-14

Carter, Jimmy, 36
Cascades Mountain Range, 64-65
Chouet, Bernard, 59
Clausen, H. B., 63
Climate, effect of ash on, 28, 63
Coldwater Lake, 70
Columbia River, 17, 37
Composite volcano, 46
Continental Drift theory, 42-43, 45
Convection currents, 45, 77
Cougar, Washington, 37
Cowlitz River, 17, 37
Craters, 10, 11, 24
Crops, effect of eruption on, 33

Dairy farming, effects of eruption on, 69

Dansgaard, Willi, 63
Death toll, 33
Debris, 18
Doukas, Mike, 31

Earthquake/volcano relationship, 41–46
Eaton, Gordon, 52
Ecological regeneration, 72
Eggers, Al, 13
Epicenter, 10, 77
Eruptions, 8, 16, 28–29, 30, 31, 32
    nonexplosive, 30–31
    previous, 3, 6
    type of, 50
Evacuation, 18
Explosion, 15, 60

Farmers, 33, 69
Fish, effect of eruption on, 17, 35, 67–72
Fissures, 45
Flood eruption, 51
Folklore, 2–3
Friatic explosion, 11, 77
Fumaroles, 23, 51, 59

Gairdner, Meredith, 3
Gases, 12, 30, 51, 52
Geological disasters, 41
Geological Survey, 31
Geothermal energy, 10, 77
Gifford Pinchot National Forest, 1, 7
Gondwanaland, 42

Harmonic tremors, 12, 29, 30
Hawaiian volcanoes, 49
Healing process, 71
Height reduction of Mount St. Helens, 24

Ignimbrite, 51, 77

Johnson, John, 73
Johnston, David, 11, 14

"Lady of Fire" (Loo-Wit), 2–3
Lahars, 17, 77
Laser, 52
Laser-reflector, 57
Laurasia, 42
Lava, 51, 77
Lava dome, 13, 29–30, 31, 32, 56–58
Legalities, 39
Leick, Robert, 39
Lithosphere, 77
Longview, Washington, 20

Magma, 11, 12, 45, 77
Malone, Steve, 60, 62
Menard, H. W., 43
Mercalli scale, 77
Meteorological disasters, 41
Mount Baker, 65
Mount Bezymianny, 61
Mount Hood, 3, 65
Mount Lassen, 64
Mount Rainier, 64, 65

Mountain range, underwater, 43
Mudflows, 17, 51
Mud river, 19

National Guard, 12
Newhall, Christopher, 55, 60
Nuées ardentes (glowing avalanches), 15, 50, 78

Patterson, John, 68
Peterson, Donald, 61
Plant life, 65, 67–72
Plate tectonics, 45, 78
Plinian volcanoes, 49
Pompeii, 49
Portland, Oregon, 39
Predicting eruptions, 52–53, 60, 62
Pumice, 50, 78
Pyroclastic fall, 50, 78
Pyroclastic flow, 17, 50–51

Ray, Dixie Lee, 12–14, 36, 40
Red Zone, 37
Richter Scale, 7, 15, 61, 78
Rift, 78
Ring of Fire, 46, 64
Ritzville, 22
Rivers, effect of eruption on, 37
Ruediger, Bill, 68

Satellites, use of in predicting eruptions, 53

Scientists, 13, 32, 51–55
Search, 26
Seismic activity, 32
Seismic tremors, 62
Seismic vibrations, 12
Seismicity, 58
Seismograph, 7, 78
Seismometer, 52, 78
Shera, Jack, 68
Shield volcanoes, 46, 49, 78
Sial, 41, 78
Sima, 41, 78
Skunk cabbage, reappearance of, 70
Spirit Lake, 13, 14, 17, 23, 24, 38
Stockbridge, Jay, 68
Strato volcanoes, 46, 78
Strombolian volcanoes, 49
Sulfuric acid theory, 63

Tambora eruption, 63
Tidal waves, 51
Tilling, Robert, 64
Tiltmeter, 52, 57, 58, 62, 78
Timber, effect of eruption on, 55
Timberline Camp, 13
Tourist business, effect on, 37, 39
Toutle River, 17, 37
Towley, Pete, 29
Truman, Harry R., 14, 23, 24, 62
Tsunamis (tidal waves), 51

U.S. Forest Service, 12, 13, 73
U.S. Geological Survey (USGS), 7, 10, 52, 53, 55, 58, 60, 61, 64, 65

Vesuvian volcanoes, 49
Volcanoes
  types of, 46, 49
  use of, 51
Volcanologists, 52
Volcanology, 55-66

Vulcanian volcanoes, 49

Weather, as cause of disasters, 41
  effects of eruption on, 28, 63
Wegener, Alfred, 42, 43, 45
White, Don, 69
Wildlife loss, 35
Wilson, J. Tuzo, 43

Yeats, Robert, 60